THE POCKET BOOK OF THE
Mustang

THE POCKET BOOK OF THE
Mustang

PETER HENSHAW

The Definitive Guide to the All American Sports Car

BARNES & NOBLE BOOKS

NEW YORK

This edition published by Barnes & Noble, Inc.,
by arrangement with Salamander Books Ltd.

2004 Barnes and Noble Books

ISBN 0-7607-5889-1

© Salamander Books Ltd., 2004

An imprint of **Chrysalis** Books Group

A CIP catalog record for this book is available from the
Library of Congress.

CREDITS
Editor: Katherine Edelston
Designer: Cara Hamilton
Reproduction: Anorax Imaging Ltd.
Production: Don Campaniello

Printed in India

Contents

Introduction

Not many cars can claim to have invented a new class of vehicle, but the Mustang did. It was, and is, a milestone car, standing alongside the Model T, the VW Beetle, the Jeep, the Mini, and the Golf Gti—all cars which had a huge effect

Below: Instantly recognisable, the Mustang's long hood and short trunk shape suggested sports car performance, but it had four seats and could be put on the road for less than $2,500.

on the public, and spawned countless imitators. On paper, the Mustang didn't look that special at all. First of all, it was a product of Detroit, not then known for its technical innovation or avant garde thinking (Chevrolet's Corsair being the honorable exception). There was nothing special about its running gear, almost all of which was plucked from existing Ford sedans. True, it had a pretty new bodyshell, but one which was no lighter, and less aerodynamic, than that of the staid Falcon it was based on. In short, the Mustang appeared to put style before content, and sceptics might have been

forgiven for thinking of it as a return to the excesses of Detroit's tailfin-happy 1950s, when style, however outrageous, impractical, or garish, came before utility.

But the Mustang wasn't like that at all. As launched, it was compact, easy to drive, and economical to run—and cheap, at a starting price of less than $2,500. It really did marry sports car looks with a measure of sedan practicality, putting the two within reach of thousands who thought they could never afford a car that looked like the Mustang. One advertising slogan (also used by the Capri, Ford Europe's very own Mustang) called it, "The Car You Always Promised Yourself." Nothing summed up the Mustang concept better than that.

1964–1966
Happy Hunting Ground

Below: The original—a 1964-1/2 Mustang coupe, (pictured here) has the optional V8, white interior, and fancy wheels.

The Ford Mustang could have been a flop—maybe not a flop on the scale of the infamous Edsel, but a flop just the same. As originally conceived, it was a sports car, a little two-seater, and the omens looked good. Ever since the Thunderbird had turned into a four-seat cruiser in 1958, enthusiasts had been pestering Ford to bring back a two-seat Thunderbird, the original "personal car." Added to which, the really committed enthusiasts had been laying down their dollars for imported sports cars for many years: MGs, Porsches, and Alfa Romeos. Apart from the Corvette, there was no other American sports car to rival them.

There were other reasons to suppose that the time was right for a new American-built sports car—simple demographics, for one. The baby boomers, those kids who had built hot rods in the 1950s, were now looking to buy their first new car. Often college educated and with high incomes, they were prime targets for car manufacturers. "Get 'em young and keep 'em for life" was a strong sales motto, and often worked out in practice.

Youth and sportiness looked like the keys to success in the 1960s. General Motors transformed the Corvair into the sporty Monza, and Plymouth was working on a fastback version of the Valiant. The first Kennedy administration had just taken office, and with the privations of the Second World War long gone, it must have seemed like anything was possible.

Right: Early Mustangs had a wide choice of engines, and most buyers opted for a V8 rather than the economy straight-six.

Below: Three things marked a Mustang interior from that of the lowly Falcon: sports steering wheel, bucket seats, floor shifter.

Above: That galloping pony would become familiar to a couple of generations of Mustang owners, and is still worn by Mustangs to this day.

The Fairlane Committee probably had the same sort of mindset when they met up, early on Saturday mornings in 1961/62. Who were they? A group of young and keen Ford executives, who found they could brainstorm better over a drink or dinner than in some committee room back at headquarters. There were six of them: Don Frey the engineer, production man Hal Sperlich, and Walter

Murphy from public relations. Sid Olsen was a copywriter and Frank Zimmerman represented marketing. And of course, there was Lee Iacocca, who at age thirty-seven was then the fastest rising star in the Ford firmament. Given the atmosphere and enthusiasm, and the mood of the times,

Above: Historically the convertibles never sold as well as the coupes, but they certainly gave "wind in the hair" fun for four.

maybe it was inevitable that their thoughts would turn to sports cars. At the time of course, Ford's top executive was Robert McNamara, whose no-nonsense approach saw the sensible, economical Falcon sedan into production. Maybe that's why the Fairlaners met at a hostelry a mile down the road from Ford headquarters—their frivolous sports car wasn't in keeping with McNamara's philosophy.

Frivolous it may have been but their two-seater did make it to the mock-up stage, and as late as 1962, it was doing the rounds as a show car, with a mid-mounted V4 engine and all-independent suspension. At customer clinics, the enthusiasts loved it, but the plain fact was, that if Ford had launched the Mustang as that mid-engined two-seater, it would, in mass production terms, have bombed.

Right: Details counted on early Mustangs, like those fake air scoops just aft of the doors. The knock-off wire wheels are fake too.

Left: Truth be told, very little hardware on the Mustang's skin was actually new. It borrowed most of its running gear from the Falcon and Fairlane sedan. So the Mustang might not have the pedigree of a Jaguar or Porsche, but you could buy one, brand new, for less than $2,500.

Above: Ford's masterstroke with the Mustang was that long hood/short deck layout, styled by Dave Ash, that gave the required suggestion of "sports car" but hid seating for four.

The truth was that sports cars in America sold in relatively small numbers—lots of people who lusted after a Corvette, an MG, or a Porsche, then went and bought a practical sedan instead.

Lee Iacocca, an instinctive salesman, could see the warning signals even at those first customer clinics, where potential customers raved over the new car: "I looked at the guys saying it," he later recalled, "the offbeat crowd, the real buffs. I said, 'That's for sure not the car we want to build, because it can't be a volume car.'" If he needed confirmation, it came from Ford's finance department.

They forecast that the mid-engined sportster would sell maybe 35,000 units a year, which was hardly worth cranking up the production lines for, let alone able to make a profit. This was Ford, and such a thing was unthinkable, so the two-seater died at that point.

Then came the masterstroke. Iacocca ordered the design team to put some extra length into the wheelbase

Below: A short deck maybe, but the Mustang still had enough luggage room to make it practical for day-to-day transport.

Previous page: Count the seats. In its original two-seat form, the Mustang would have sold less, just like the Chevrolet's Corvette, or Ford's own original Thunderbird. The inclusion of four seats broadened its appeal hugely.

Right: Like it or not, there would never have been a Mustang without the Falcon, Ford's economy sedan that sold by the thousand in the early 1960s, though this 327 Shaker has left its budget roots far behind.

and add two rear seats. The uncompromising sports car was transformed into what he described as "small-sporty," a sporty looking family car, but practical and glamorous at the same time. Along the way, it acquired a conventional

Below: A 1965 fastback added to the Mustang's appeal, though it never matched coupe sales.

front engine/rear drive layout, which meant it could make maximum use of existing Ford components. So it would be relatively quick and cheap to develop, and to build. To maximize sales, it would have to be cheap, and the target was set at a base price of just $2,500, with a weight of 2,500 lb. So the "small-sporty" was a small car by Detroit standards, but it might just sell in Detroit numbers. The finance guys predicted 100,000 a year. Iacocca (who dismissed them as "bean counters") reckoned on 200,000. As it turned out, both estimates were way too low.

But they still weren't out of the woods yet, as Henry Ford II had the final say on all new models. It was a tough call, as the company was planning to spend a lot of money to retool its entire line for 1965, so it was a difficult time to talk of a new car. Not only that, but the boss had long had an uneasy relationship with Iacocca, who he suspected of having designs on the top job. But after endless meetings (along with some carefully planted rumours inside the company and the motoring press) Iacocca's famous salesmanship won through, and the "small-sporty" project was on.

It was the summer of 1962, and Ford engineers had just twenty-one months to turn a concept into a production-ready car. Even the styling hadn't been finalized, so to speed things up a little, styling chief Gene Bordinat held a competition—his top men had two weeks to come up with full-size clay mock-ups, the winner would go into production. In the event, the choice was easy, as the Dave Ash-designed car, with its classic long-hood/short-trunk proportions, looked right from the start.

Development was relatively easy, given that engines, transmissions, suspension, and even much of the interior

Above: This is what persuaded many of those thousands of customers to buy a Mustang—a sporty looking interior.

Opposite and right: A 1965 289 Hi-Po Mustang— if things had been different, the Mustang would have been called Cougar, minus the pony.

Above: A neat rear end treatment typified all the early Mustangs—it looks relatively weak compared to later cars.

would come straight off the Ford parts shelf, chiefly from the Falcon and Fairlane sedans. Only the body was genuinely new. There were some minor glitches, especially concerning the car's low hood line—both air-cleaner and radiator cap had to be redesigned so that they would squeeze underneath—but work proceeded quickly. The

Top right: This is the top of the range 289 Hi-Po coupe, the hottest Mustang available in the early days.

"small-sporty" just needed one more thing, a name. Many within the company nicknamed it the "Special Falcon" as it used so many Falcon parts. Officially, the project name was "Cougar" which a lot of people wanted to use in production. Henry Ford II favored "T-Bird II;" others liked "Torino." But in the event, one name won hands down. It had all the right connotations of American muscle, freedom, and wide open spaces—it was the Mustang.

Sensational Launch

When it was finally launched in April 1964, the Mustang caused a sensation. No one had seen anything quite like it before. Here was a car that looked exotic and sporty, yet came with the amazingly low base price of $2,368. It looked great in the driveway, yet was easy to drive and cheap to run. It had the essential sporty car cues like a stickshift, three-spoke steering wheel, and bucket seats, yet could be serviced by any Ford dealer. And it had four seats,

Below: A 1965 289 coupe, with a softer V8 than the ultimate Hi-Po, though here with four-speed transmission.

Right: Ford named the fastback a 2+2, which was an honest label as the sloping roof restricted room in the back.

so it was practical for families, as long as the kids weren't too lanky or numerous.

No wonder that crowds gathered outside Ford dealers. Fueled up by a massive advertising campaign, they were able to see and touch a real Mustang in every local Ford dealer on launch day, and that in itself was a marketing masterstroke. Four million people walked through showroom doors to take a look over that first weekend, and 22,000 actually ordered cars on the first day! One dealer found himself fielding fifteen orders for the same car—he sold it to the highest bidder.

The orders began to pile up, and to keep up with demand, Ford had to switch a second factory over to

Left: This is a 1965 Mustang, which despite appearances is actually a coupe, not a convertible with the ragtop in place. Its vinyl roof just gives that impression. This car also features non-standard wheels.

Mustang production, then a third. At one point there was a three-month waiting list, and to prove just how strong the pent-up demand was, Frank Zimmerman offered Ford dealers in Dayton, Ohio, all the Mustangs they wanted—in short order, the car had taken ten percent of the entire local market, an astonishing feat for a single model. So

maybe it's not quite so surprising that over 417,000 Mustangs were sold in the first twelve months, making it the fastest selling car of all time. Lee Iacocca, the Fairlane Committee, and the "bean counters" could all relax—the Mustang was a smash hit. Of course, if all those thousands of buyers had paid just $2,368 for their new Mustang,

Below: Not visible in this shot, but this 1965 fastback has the optional Pony Interior, the first of many optional upgrades.

Ford would have barely made a profit on the whole project. The ads hadn't lied; you really could drive out of a Ford showroom in a new Mustang hardtop, having written a check for that amount. However, it would have had the Falcon's weak six-cylinder engine under the hood, mustering just 170 cu. in., 101 hp, and 156 lb. ft. Bearing in mind that the Mustang actually weighed more than a

Below: This fastback features the four-speed manual transmission—an option which was available from 1965, though many customers opted for the automatic.

Falcon and its aerodynamics were no better, the result was no tarmac burning muscle car. The basic Mustang was also hampered by a three-speed transmission (with no syncromesh on first gear), skinny tires, drum brakes, soft suspension, and low-geared steering. It is little wonder that one journalist described the result as, "about as exciting as a dish of baby food."

Inside, the dashboard consisted of the Falcon's economy strip speedometer—there were no extra dials and very little to suggest that this was a sporty car. Of course, from the outside it looked just as good as any other Mustang, sitting shiny in the driveway, but as a driving experience, the basic car was underwhelming.

So not many people bought the basic model, but one of the Mustang's most attractive features was the sheer choice it offered. The sports car looks and that bargain-basement price lured folk into the showroom, but once they were there, Ford salesmen could start playing the options game. There were four engines to choose from, and seven transmissions; four braking systems, four wheel types, and three steering set-ups, plus a whole host of minor items, from a radio to whitewall tires, and the "Rally Pac" (combined tachometer and clock). And of course, if you didn't fancy the hardtop Mustang, there was always the convertible, and from 1965 a fastback as well. Few buyers could resist adding a few goodies to their Mustang, and every single option they bought boosted Ford's profit margin. So the Mustang didn't only sell well, it made money too.

Let's take a closer look at the engine options. The first step up from that Falcon six was a 260 cu. in. V8, straight out of the Fairlane, and offering (in mild two-barrel

Below: This "K-code" 1965
convertible has the full
Hi-Po 271 hp 289 V8—most
buyers preferred the
milder version.

carburetor form) 164 hp at 4,400 rpm, and 258 lb. ft. at 2,200. If that wasn't enough, a 289 cu. in. version of the same engine offered 210 hp, helped along by a single four-barrel carb and higher 9.0:1 compression. But for eager drivers, there could only be one choice, the "Hi-Po" 289, though this wasn't available for the first two months of

Mustang production. With 271 hp, this took the car into serious performance territory. It had a 10.5:1 compression, low-restriction air-cleaner, a high-lift cam with mechanical lifters, and individual headers for the exhaust. Internally, it was radically beefed-up, with a cross-bolted crankcase and high-tensile con-rods.

Following page: 1966, and final year for the original Mustang, before it began to grow to accommodate big-block V8s. Badging was discrete on this 289 V8.

Opposite top: The five-dial instrument pack, pictured here, was an option from 1965. It finally banished that Falcon speedometer—there was still no standard tachometer though.

Opposite bottom: In restored Mustangs the engine bay presentation is just as important as the bodywork.

Above: This is a 1966 GT convertible automatic featuring all the GT extras. These were only available on 225 hp and 271 hp V8 Mustangs.

Ticking the Hi-Po box also brought a four-speed manual transmission, so it wasn't a cheap option, at $442. And in fact, very few Mustang buyers chose it. Comfort and convenience items, like automatic transmission and air-conditioning, together with one of the softer V8s, were far

Opposite: This is a 1966
GT convertible. The GT
pack consisted of a
handling suspension
package, front disc brakes,
dual exhaust, the five-dial
instrument set, stripes,
badges, and spot lights.

more popular. In fact, let's be blunt, the early Mustang was
in no way a performance car. Its soft suspension (even the
optional harder set-up) came straight out of the Falcon and
Fairlane, and it would always be hampered by leaf rear
springs on a live axle. The steering (three and a half turns
lock to lock) was slow by sports car standards, and the

Right: This 1966
convertible GT has the
four-barrel 225 hp 289-
power unit—not as hot as
the Hi-Po, but giving useful
performance nonetheless.

Right: A pretty 1966 coupe, built at a time when the Mustang faced no real opposition, one reason why 1966 was its best year ever, with over 600,000 cars sold.

standard drum brakes did not inspire confidence. But that wasn't the point. The Mustang looked like a performance car, which was why thousands of folk bought it in 1965, while just 1.3 percent of them paid extra for a Hi-Po. In any case, more serious Mustangs were waiting just over the horizon.

Carroll Shelby was the man who brought these cars to life. The retired chicken farmer and race driver had a good track record—he had created the legendary AC Cobra, marrying a Ford 260 V8 with the lightweight English sports car, to create the most exhilarating road car of them all. Now Iacocca asked him to perform the same trick with the Mustang. Ostensibly, it was all about racing—Shelby was contracted to build 100 special Mustangs to qualify it for SCCA classes. In reality, five years of Shelby Mustangs proved a huge image booster to the whole range.

Mind you, those first cars, the GT 350s, where seriously hot items, designed with weekend racing in mind. To cut weight, a fiberglass hood was fitted, the rear seat ditched, and the stock exhaust replaced by a side muffler. Underneath, there were stiffer springs and Koni adjustable shocks, a thicker front anti-roll bar, and traction bars, plus front disc brakes and a "Monte Carlo" bracing bar between the front shock towers, to beef the bodyshell up. As for the V8, the standard Hi-Po was treated to an aluminum intake manifold, sump, and valve covers; there were Tri-Y exhaust headers, low-restriction mufflers, and a bigger 751 cfm Holley four-barrel carb.

The result, said Shelby, was 306 hp, which road tests appeared to confirm with a 0–60 mph time of 6.5 seconds. Here was the first true Mustang performance car, though it needed a firm hand. The Shelby was noisy and bumpy,

Below: Four-barrel Holleys sprout through the hood of this 1966 289 coupe.

even crude in some ways (especially in the way water sprayed inside through holes cut in the floor for the new suspension arms). But it was a highly effective racecar, and despite a price tag of $4,400, Shelby's Californian factory

turned out 500 of them. The Mustang might be a legend, but the Shelby variant surely qualifies as a sub-legend in its own right.

Meanwhile, Ford was making its own changes to the standard Mustang for 1965. Although demand was still running high, and the company had got ahead of the competition (meaning GM and Chrysler), it wouldn't be long before Mustang rivals began to appear—in the meantime, the original ponycar had to be kept fresh with regular updates. With that in mind the fastback Mustang was introduced that year, with a rakish rear end and a fold-down rear seat to increase luggage room. It was more of a 2+2 than a full four-seater, but added greatly to the Mustang's appeal.

Above: The full GT equipment on a 1966 black coupe—many Mustang buyers liked to combine the show-off parts with a mild motor.

Opposite: By contrast, non-GT Mustangs (like this 1966 coupe) looked a little plain—it was amazing what a set of stripes, wheels, and spotlights could do.

There were power increases all round too—maybe Ford feared that the Mustang might gain a reputation as a fake, all for show, no go. Whatever the reason, that Falcon straight-six was ditched in favor of a 200 cu. in. unit offering 120 hp—it was a great success, and soon one in three Mustang customers was choosing the six-cylinder option. The 260 cu. in. V8 was dropped in favor of a detuned two-barrel 289, which had a torquey 200 hp, and the standard 289 was pushed up to 225 hp. The Hi-Po stayed at 271 hp, but again only a few buyers chose it. More popular was the new GT option package, which brought together many of the performance items. Available with the 225 hp and 271 hp V8s only, this offered the Handling suspension package (stiffer springs and shocks, a thicker anti-roll bar and slightly quicker steering) front disc brakes, dual exhaust, and a new five-dial instrument pack, plus stripes, badges, and front lights. If you didn't want to

Left: The Mustang's best year (sales wise) was 1966, when this red coupe left the production line. Nearly half of its buyers stuck with the basic six-cylinder motor, though this now offered 120 hp, enough for reasonable performance.

Below: This is a 1966 GT
convertible 289—a nice
combination in red with a
white top.

show off, the GT package could be had without stripes.
And if this all seemed too "road-racer," a new luxury
interior, with galloping pony motifs on the seats, simulated
wood trim, and the five-dial instruments, was another new
option on offer.

Below: This is a 1966 GT convertible 289—a nice combination in red with a white top.

For Ford, 1966 was the final year of the Mustang's happy hunting ground. Until late 1966, it faced no real opposition. Plymouth's Barracuda was nice, but not in the same class, and it wasn't until late that year that GM's ponycars, the Chevrolet Camaro and Pontiac Firebird,

Opposite and below:
Seen here is an automatic
coupe from 1966, by which
time the five-dial
instrument pack was
standard on all Mustangs,
along with rear seat belts,
a padded dashboard, and
hazard flashers.

were launched. Maybe that's why the 1966 model year was
Mustang's best ever, with well over 600,000 cars sold. The
millionth Mustang rolled off the line that year too. It was
not a lie when Ford claimed that it had built the three
fastest-selling cars of all time: the Model A, the Falcon, and
now the Mustang.

There was something else behind burgeoning Mustang
sales in 1966. Car sales in general were falling, in part
thanks to the economic effects of the Vietnam War, as
interest rates rose and buying power declined. In these
harder times, the Mustang was pushed as a compact
economy car, and compared to most Detroit sedans, that's

Previous page and left:
This is not a genuine
Shelby, despite the
stripes—there were no
Shelby coupes, only
fastbacks and
convertibles.

Below: 1966 was the final
year for the original
Mustang engine lineup,
with a small-block 289 as
the flagship.

exactly what it was. One ad stressed the six-cylinder
ponycar's fuel economy ("Now don't forget to wave when
you pass your gas station!") and a special edition Mustang
Sprint combined the six with stripes, wheel covers, a center
console, and chrome air-cleaner.

So nearly half those 600,000 Mustangs (forty-two
percent) were ordered with a six-cylinder engine instead of
the V8, while all Mustangs now came with the five-dial
instrument pack, plus safety items like front and rear seat
belts, a padded dashboard, and hazard flashers. There were

even signs that the Shelby GT 350 was going soft. It had been a great image booster, but sales were limited by the GT's uncompromising character. So for 1966, the suspension was softened a little, and the noisy, clunky Detroit Lock limited-slip differential dropped altogether. The result was quieter and softer, less likely to win races but less challenging to drive to the office. As if to underline the fact, a radio and automatic transmission became options, as did a whole range of colors—the original GT

Above: Hottest of the hot—a Shelby GT 350 in its original colors, white with blue stripes.

Opposite top and bottom: Carroll Shelby claimed 306 hp for the GT 350, a useful increase.

Left: Imagine it . . . twenty-one years old, $20, and a driver's license—all you needed to rent a Shelby GT 350 from Hertz for the day. Make it a weekend and expect to get some Saturday night racing in!

Above: Only Shelby fastbacks had that distinctive rear three-quarter window—the 2005 Mustang apes it.

350 had been any color you liked, as long as it was white with blue racing stripes. And while the new, more polite Shelby Mustang might not win any races, it was $100 cheaper than the first one—sales increased four-fold.

The Shelby Mustang profile was aided no end by the infamous Hertz GT 350s. Hard to believe now, but Hertz

really did buy 1,000 of the hottest Mustangs available, to rent to anyone who could afford the $17 a day rental. Not surprisingly, many of the GT 350Hs (built especially for Hertz) were quickly worn out or written off by weekend racers, whether the racing involved was officially on the drag strip or unofficially on the road. Those Mustangs would have cost Hertz a lot more to purchase and maintain than the average Falcon, but the whole idea garnered huge publicity, which worked for Ford too, as thousands of drivers had a chance to try out the hot Mustang, and some of them subsequently bought one.

But the Hertz Mustangs marked the end of an era. From the 1967 model year, Ford's ponycar would face a whole new generation of rivals. It wouldn't have the market to itself any more.

Right: Stock Shelbys didn't come with fancy wheels like the ones seen here, just widened Ford items.

1967–1968
Gaining Girth

Below: A 1967 fastback in café setting—shove a coin in the jukebox, slide behind the wheel, and dream.

Ford might have invented the ponycar, but its very success attracted rivals. As well as GM's Camaro and Firebird, there was a reborn Barracuda and AMC's Javelin and AMX. But as always, it was big General Motors that came with most muscle. Not just financial muscle either, as a prime design aim for both the Camaro and Firebird was to offer more cubic inches and horsepower than the Mustang. And they succeeded—the top 396 and 400 cu. in. V8 options made a Hi-Po look distinctly weak. Ford had big-block V8s that could mount a credible response, but they were physically too large to fit the Mustang.

So the car itself was expensively redesigned. To make its engine bay big enough to accept a big-block, the Mustang was widened by three inches, with an extra two inches on

each track and another couple on the length. Outwardly, it took a keen eye to notice the difference, though Iacocca thought the original Mustang concept of a lightweight, sporty car had been betrayed—he described the 1967 car as, "more like a fat pig," than the original "sleek horse."

The horse had certainly gained some girth, tipping the scales at 130 lb. heavier than its predecessor. However, the larger engine bay did allow Ford to slot in its 390 cu. in.

Below: A 1967 GT fastback—note that the teardrop hood is not original!

V8, which at $264 extra looked like very good value. *Car and Driver* magazine tested a Mustang 390, and pointed out that the heavy big-block V8 meant that the extra weight was carried over the front wheels. But despite this front-heavy weight distribution (60/40 front/rear) they were surprised at how well the 390 handled. It had, wrote the testers, "balance and handling . . . it's very hard to throw it off balance." *Car and Driver* also reckoned that

Below: A 1967 GT-equipped 390 V8 coupe, looking elegant in black with no vinyl roof.

Left and below: A shining example of a 1967 289 convertible automatic. Just because a big-block V8 was optional, didn't make it compulsory.

Below: Slightly softer than before, but the GT 350 Shelby still meant business, as the monstrous spotlights suggest.

this was the fastest ponycar in a straight line—the automatic tested produced a 15.2-second quarter-mile. That year, readers of *Car and Driver* voted for the 390 as the best sports sedan over 300 cu. in.

If there was a honeymoon period for the Mustang 390, that was it. When *Hot Rod*'s Eric Dahlquist tested one, he

Left: A 1967 fastback—bigger all round, but the changes to Lee Iaccoca's "fat pig" were actually quite subtle.

Below: A 289 (as featured in this fastback with power steering) wasn't the flagship Mustang any more.

Above: For those of a retiring disposition, the GT package could be had without the stripes and badges, as on this 1967 fastback.

liked it, but his performance figures made the 390 a whole half-second slower over the quarter than a Camaro 350 (let alone the full-house 396). Later in the year Dean Gregson of veteran dealer Tasca Ford told Dahlquist the blunt truth about the 390. "We sold a lot of 390 Mustangs last fall and into winter," he said, "but by March they dropped off to practically nothing. We found the car so non-competitive we began to feel we were cheating the customer." Worse was to come. *Car and Driver* may have liked that first 390, but it had changed its collective mind

Above: On the other hand, some people wanted the world to know about their GT-equipped Mustang.

Opposite: Bigger it might be, but the 1967 Mustang had exactly the same proportions as the original.

Left: Only two years after it first appeared, the GT 350 Shelby had compromised its race-bred heart a little, become softer and easier to live with, though (as this 1967 example shows) it still looked the part of a race-ready roadster.

Above: Shelby beat Ford to the production of a 428 big-block Mustang—in the GT 500—though it was never as hairy as the original 350.

Opposite top: More fiberglass scoops and spoilers on the 1967 Shelby, though the hood scoops were relatively subtle.

Right: Glinting in the evening sun. The difference was that a GT 500 would cruise you comfortably across a State or two before sunset.

Below: Big-block power gave the Shelby GT 500 a claimed 355 hp and 420 lb. ft., making it the most powerful production Mustang so far.

Right: Performance? The owner of this 1967 GT 500 fastback could expect 0–60 mph in 6.5 seconds, and a fifteen-second quarter-mile.

by March 1968, when it tested a GT 390 fastback against a Camaro 396, Firebird 400, Mercury Cougar XR-7 (Ford's own luxury Mustang), Barracuda Formula S, and a Javelin SST. The magazine used its usual points scoring system in a multi-test, the top car in each category scoring six points, the lowest, one point. Overall, the Firebird came out tops, with 118 points, and the Mustang trailed in last, with just seventy-three. In fact, it was awarded the lowest score in servicing, steering effort, brake fade, trunk space,

Below: Automatic transmission plus GT equipment equaled the short-lived GTA in 1967, in fastback (as here) or open top form.

visibility, and a whole list of other things. The 390 V8 wasn't all it should have been either, and *Car and Driver* scathingly ranked its acceleration, "in the lame gazelle class." Oddly enough, despite the poor points showing, the Mustang did better on subjective impressions, but it was clear that the original ponycar just hadn't kept up with the

younger competition. "Ford," concluded *Car and Driver*,
"has been content to rest on its laurels."

But for Mustang lovers who wanted a big-cube answer
to Chevrolet and Pontiac, there was hope. Tasca Ford,
after being less than polite about the 390, got up and did
something about it. Ford's own 428 cu. in. V8 was the
same physical size as the 390, so it would slot straight
under the latest Mustang's hood. Tasca Ford did just that,
and began producing Mustang KR ("King of the Road")
specials in the summer of 1967. The 428 came in Police
Interceptor form, which brought big-valve heads, a

Above: A pretty blue
coupe in 1968 trim, by
which time the 289 V8
hardly qualified for muscle
car status. The big-block
390, and later the 428,
took care of that.

Above: Look closely, and there's the proof that this is the first of the factory-built big-block Mustangs, the 1968 390, which Ford hoped would play catch up in the horsepower wars.

Left: Ford fans were excited by the arrival of the first 390 cu. in. Mustang, and early road tests heaped praise on the car. But it was soon left behind by more muscular rivals.

Below: A rare High Country Special from 1967. Just 300 of these limited editions were built, for Denver Ford dealers. It was very similar in specification to the California Special.

735 cfm four-barrel Holley carb, and 335 horsepower—and it could rocket the Mustang KR over the quarter-mile in 13.39 seconds.

The KR of course, was a dealer special, so it was produced in very small numbers. But months before, Shelby announced its own big-cube Mustang, the 428-engined GT 500. Available in fastback or convertible form (there were no Shelby hardtops), it claimed to pack a respectable 355 hp at 5,400 rpm and 420 lb. ft. at

Right: This red convertible shows the plain grille and steel wheels that identify 1968 Mustangs, plus yet another variation on the fake rear vent.

Below: Scoops aplenty on this 1968 Shelby GT 500—Shelby customers now had a choice of colors as well, a change from the "white or nothing" original.

Below and right:
Encouraged by Tasca
Ford's big-block Mustang
special, and the GT 500,
Ford lost only a little time
in slotting the 428 cu. in.
V8 into its own production-
line car.

3,200 rpm, so when *Car and Driver* tested one, they expected a rip-roaring performance. They were disappointed. Well, maybe disappointed isn't the right word. Sure, the GT 500 only turned in a fifteen-second quarter-mile, but as *Car and Driver* pointed out, it was just as fast as the original GT 350, but much more civilized. "A grown up sports car for smooth touring," was how they summed it up.

Below: Looking almost Italian from this angle, the GT 500 Shelby remained the most powerful Mustang for 1968, claiming 355 hp against the Cobra Jet's 335 hp.

Could they really be describing a Shelby? Yes they could, because the hottest Mustangs were being civilized and softened as the years went by. The deluxe interior was standard now, as was a fold-down rear seat, power steering, and power brakes. There were macho looking fiberglass body parts, but less serious hardware under the hood. So the Shelby continued its transition from barely tamed racer to a look-at-me special. But did anyone really care? The price came down and sales went up, while the GT 500, for a while, had more cubes than any other ponycar, civilized or not.

As 1968 came along it was in the midst of the muscle car boom, when anyone could walk into their nearest Chrysler or Chevy showroom and drive out at the wheel of

Above: A 1968 California Special Mustang, an idea put together by southern California Ford dealers, combining some Shelby body parts with the six-cylinder engine.

Right: Nearly 4,000 California Specials were built, all with extra stripes, scoops, a rear spoiler, and Thunderbird sequential rear turn signals.

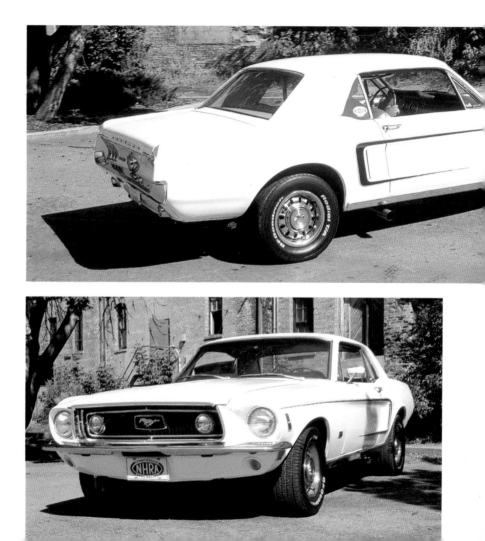

a 400 horsepower V8, and the biggest-engined production Mustang ever was rolling off the production line.

Yet the basic six-cylinder ponycar lived on, and thousands of folk bought them. Not just Mustangs but Camaros and Barracudas as well, all playing the same role of good looking and economical compact. Most road tests concentrated on the big V8s, because that's what the hot car fans wanted to read about, but *Motor Trend* did compare the Mustang, Camaro, and Barracuda sixes at least once. Ford's entry-level ponycar had been derated to 115 hp, but the testers thought it was the pick of this bunch. Unlike its rivals, it used smaller brakes and lighter running gear, instead of the full-house V8 equipment, so it weighed 300 lb. less than either of them. So despite less power, it could keep up with the Chevy and Plymouth, and used less fuel in the process. The six-cylinder Mustang even came in its own special editions for 1968. Both the California Special and High Country Special came with

Above: Mustang GTs looked quite plain for 1968, at least compared to a Shelby or California Special The styled steel wheels were fitted that year only.

Opposite and right: This 1968 GT is fitted with a big-block 428, though externally it looks identical to the 390 it overshadowed.

Above: A 1968 High Country Special, identical to the California Special except for its name and badging.

Shelby-like add-ons: rear spoiler, blacked-out front grille, special badges, and GT-style wheels. And at $2,602 for the basic hardtop, the six-cylinder Mustang was faithful to its affordable roots.

But while these bread and butter ponycars kept on selling, most attention was grabbed by the latest V8. Ford had evidently been listening to all that stuff about the 390 being a little inadequate next to more muscular ponycars, and for 1968 it followed the example of both Shelby and Tasca Ford, launching its own 428-engined car. Not that

Above: A 1968 coupe GT automatic, with the 302 cu. in. V8.

Left: The younger 302 would finally replace the faithful 289, which made its first appearance in the Boss 302.

this was the first 428 Mustang to hail from a Ford production line. Truth be told, the GT 500 Shelby was actually built by the blue oval itself. Then it was shipped to the Shelby plant in California for finned aluminum valve covers and a new air filter to be bolted on, plus all the fiberglass bodywork and a roll cage. Those Shelby badges were more of a marketing operation than an indication of who had built the car.

But no matter, as Ford's own Cobra Jet Mustang stormed in and swept aside all of the criticisms after a few acceleration runs. "Get away from that bridge," wrote John Raffat in *Car Craft* magazine, aiming his words at despairing Ford fans. "Throw away your razor blades and dump out the strychnine!" What Raffat was trying to say was that here at last was a performance Ford for the fans, straight from the factory, that would need no apology. Ford, it's true, had taken a while to really tag on to the

Left: Meanwhile, the 289 was still available, though long since overshadowed by the big-block Mustangs.

Above: A nice 1968 fastback in Brittany Blue, with the distinctive wheels and coach striping used that year.

Following page: The High Country and California Specials offered some of the kudos of a Shelby, without the running costs.

Pictured here is an agressive-looking red and black example of a 1968 High Country Special.

Opposite: But those mean looking scoops did actually serve a purpose, the uppers were there to extract interior air, the lowers to cool the rear brakes.

Below: For midyear 1968, the GT 500 became the GT 500 KR (for "King of the Road") echoing the original Tasca Ford 428 Mustang.

Above: For 1968, the Shelby GT 500 was still big-block 428 powered, but quoted power had slipped down to 335 hp, the same as the standard Mustang Cobra Jet, and the Shelby emphasis was increasingly on appearance, not performance.

Left: Aftermarket wheels on this fastback GT, which hides a 428 Cobra Jet under the hood, the engine that put it back into muscle car contention.

Below: If the 428 seemed too much, then you could still order a 1968 Mustang with the 390, this one in a fastback GT.

muscle car movement, but now it was up there with a vengeance.

The question was could the Cobra Jet justify all this hype? The signs were good—it had twenty-eight more cubic inches than a Firebird 400, and weighed 260 lb. less. *Hot Rod* tried one, and recorded a 13.56-second standing quarter, at over 106 mph, plus 0–60mph in 5.9 seconds. That made it faster than a Firebird, any Firebird. Eric Dahlquist declared it to be, "probably the fastest regular production sedan ever built . . . A single Cobra Jet blast-off will send thousands into orbit for the nearest auto loan department."

Below: Ford claimed 325 hp for the 390 V8, not enough to make this Mustang a top-line muscle car.

Maybe Carroll Shelby didn't want to be upstaged by all of this, maybe he was bored, but in 1968 not all Shelby Mustangs were body kit specials. The GT 350 was still on offer, though now with Ford's latest 302 cu. in. V8 replacing the 289. This produced 250 hp in standard form, which looked pale in comparison with a Camaro Z28, but there were plenty of tune-up parts available. One $700 package brought big-valve heads, a sky-high 11.0:1

Left: Even while everyone was talking about 390s and 428s, plenty of Mustang buyers still opted for the economical straight six. This is a 1968 six-cylinder coupe.

Above: A convertible Shelby joined the range that same year, and this is a GT 500 KR—the roll bar was standard on open-top Shelbys.

compression (these were the days of high-octane pump fuel), aluminum intake manifold, 715 cfm Holley four-barrel, and longer duration cam timing. You could even have a limited-slip differential as well, plus a stiffer rear suspension set-up with anti-wind-up leaves. Shelby claimed 315 hp for this return to the good old days of hot and hairy GT 350s, though if that wasn't enough he also

Above: Little change at the rear for 1968, though GT Mustangs now sported four tailpipes instead of two—the real difference was under the hood.

Right: Mustang 428 CJ. *Hot Rod* magazine tested one of these soon after the 428 option appeared, and declared it "the fastest running pure stock in the history of man."

Right: Full instrumentation, with a tachometer at last, was now a standard fixture—the Mustang had come a long way since its early spartan days.

Right: Officially, the 428 cu. in. Cobra Jet delivered 335 hp, but some estimates put it closer to 375–400 hp. Whatever the true figure, it was plenty to compete with the most muscular opposition.

Left: The Cobra Jet option was introduced on April 1 1968, making this a "1968-1/2" Mustang. It was only produced in this form for a few months, until the new 1969 Mustangs took over.

Left: The 1968 302 GT fastback, far from being the performance Mustang now, but with a good balance of performance and running costs—not everyone could afford a 428!

Below: By now a tilt steering wheel (not fitted to this car) was optional, offering nine different positions, and automatically swinging up and away when the driver's door was opened, to ease access.

Top left: This is a 1968 J-code fastback, with the 302 Windsor that would become the entry-level Mustang V8.

Left and above:
Shelby GT 500 KR
convertible, from 1968,
with standard roll bar and
limited luggage room!

offered a supercharged version with an alleged 335 hp. *Road & Track* pitted a GT 350 against its arch-rival, the Z28, and concluded that the Camaro was actually the better car—better steering, better handling, and cheaper. Maybe too good to be an untamed hot rod, though.

Left: "KR" ("King of the Road") side stripes meant that this Shelby packed the 428 Cobra Jet under the hood, making it one of the fastest-accelerating road cars of its time—in 1968, muscle cars were all about straight-line get up and go.

1969–1970
Count Those Engines

Below: Lee Iacocca thought the 1967/68 Mustang had grown fat—for 1969, the Mustang grew fatter still.

For 1969, there were more Mustangs than ever before. Not in sales, which had been declining steadily since that 1966 peak, but in the number of engines on offer. Ford had Semon E. Knudsen to thank for this. Knudsen (better known as "Bunkie") was an ex-General Motors manager brought in by Henry Ford II. This had two results: one, a disgruntled Lee Iacocca, who thought he was in line for the top executive job (and he had good reason, for Detroit executives very rarely switched allegiances at the time); and secondly a wide range of Mustangs, which attempted to cover every market niche in true General Motors style.

Not only were there more Mustangs, but they were all bigger and heavier too. The basic proportions were still

**Previous page: Shelbys
adopted the wider, longer
1969 bodywork, though
mechanically little was
changed, with both the
GT 350 and 500 (as here)
continuing.**

there, but the whole car was restyled, with a new
SportsRoof which replaced the old fastback. The wheelbase
was still 108 inches, but the 1969 Mustang was four inches
longer, with a more radically raked windscreen, and a
lower roofline.

So what were the new choices? Well, there were two
sixes now, a 155 hp 250 cu. in. unit squeezing in alongside

Opposite: The Shelby trademarks were still there from 1968—the rear spoiler, fiberglass scoops, the stripes. Those gaping exhaust outlets were new.

Right: Another Shelby trademark, the Cobra poised to strike.

Below: Shock! The GT 500 was no longer the most powerful Mustang you could buy—the Boss 429 now offered 375 hp, if not more.

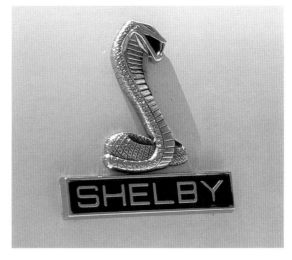

the faithful 115 hp 200. The entry-level V8 was a mild two-barrel version of the 302, with 220 hp, while a hotter four-barrel cousin powered the new Boss 302 (with 290 hp). If the customer opted for a mid-range Mustang, the choice was between the Windsor and Cleveland 351 cu. in. V8, offering 250 or 290 hp respectively. For a little more power, you could even have the 390 as well, though this older unit was only offered for a year. Given the success of the 428 Cobra Jet, this continued, now in base 335 hp

Above: Count those intakes—excluding the front grille, there were seven on every Shelby. Hood locking pins were another hot car cue of the time.

Right: The 1969 Mustang retained the original 108-inch wheelbase, as on this Shelby GT 350, but was longer overall.

Above: SportsRoof was the latest name for the fastback, now lower and with more radical rake than ever before. Basic models sold better than the fancy ones.

form or as the 360 hp Super. And finally, topping the range off in horsepower, cubic inches, and sheer kudos, was the Boss 429—of which many thought its official 375 hp was a conservative estimate.

Of the new Mustangs for 1969, the Boss brothers were probably the biggest news or, at least, they gained the most media attention. They were a statement of intent, that Ford

Above: With that lower SportsRoof, the Mustang was always a 2+2 rather than a full four-seater.

Left: Visibility was aided by a small additional rear window, but even this fastback Mustang still had a big blindspot.

Above: Look at me! The Mach 1 was the show-off Mustang for 1969— spoilers, stripes, matt black hood, and spotlights.

Opposite top: Altogether plainer is this 1969 convertible, though it too could be ordered with the 428 Cobra Jet.

Right: The plate gives this Mach 1 away as being 428 CJ-powered—fast, but a nose-heavy understeerer.

Left: The Mach 1 looked a little less macho in all-black guise, but only a little. It effectively replaced the GT option as the mainstream sporty Mustang, though a Boss 429 could outperform it.

had no intention of getting left behind in the horsepower war, and that it was serious about racing. Why? Because they were homologation specials, built in limited numbers in order for them to qualify for racing—the Boss 302 for Trans Am and the 429 for NASCAR.

The NASCAR rules stated that 500 engines had to be built to qualify, but they weren't fussy about which car they were sold in. So although Ford was campaigning the Torino in NASCAR, it could sell the qualifier motors in Mustangs. The 429 V8 certainly was a special one, so close in cubic inches to the existing 428, but completely different. The aluminum hemi heads carried O-ring head gaskets and 2.3-inch diameter intake valves, with 1.9-inch exhausts. And the motor itself was physically big—to squeeze it under the Mustang's hood, engineers had to move the front shock towers outwards by an inch. Ford claimed 375 hp for its most powerful Mustang ever, but there's little doubt that they were being modest (a not unusual ploy for any manufacturer, where race-bound engines were concerned). *Car Life* recorded a 14.09-second quarter-mile, and reckoned the true horsepower figure was more like 400 hp. The Boss 429's brutal horsepower made it a highly effective drag-strip machine, though the magazine actually found it to be better behaved in traffic than the street-orientated Mach 1.

Left: Had the 1969 Shelby gone soft? Brock Yates of *Car and Driver* magazine certainly thought so when he tried a GT 350 (this is a 500 SportsRoof).

Below: "Little more than a tough looking Mustang Grande," he wrote, "a Thunderbird for Hells Angels. Certainly not the car of Carroll Shelby's dreams."

So if the Boss 429 was all about straight-line speed and acceleration to suit the oval tracks of NASCAR, what of its little brother? The 302 Boss was quite different in character, with that small-block 302 V8 tuned up as a high-revver. The high-lift camshaft and 780 cfm Holley might have been expected, but the crankshaft was statically and dynamically balanced, to make the motor happy at high revs. Officially, the rev limit was 5,800 rpm, but some owners said that useful power carried on to 8,000 (if you

ditched the rev limiter). As it was heading for the twistier tracks of Trans Am, the Boss 302 was lowered, with heavy-duty suspension and seven-inch wide wheels.

A Boss 302 could be used on the road, but its real purpose was to meet and beat the Camaro Z28 on the track so there were countless magazine duels between the

Above: A 1969 Mach 1 390. For a short while, you could still order a Mustang with the 390 V8, but most big-block customers preferred the ultimate 428.

Below: If a stock Mach 1 wasn't wild enough, buyers could order a standout rear spoiler, or that louver cover for the rear window.

two cars. *Car and Driver* first found that the Boss was slightly slower than a Z28 over the quarter-mile, but nearly half a second quicker around Lime Rock racetrack, so it handled well. But the Boss Mustangs were expensive and specialized, and for anyone not heading for competition (or with a slightly slimmer wallet) the Mustang of choice was

Above: This is a 1969 Mach 1 shorn of all add-on parts, apart from a set of modern alloy wheels, still with that unmistakable ponycar profile.

Previous page: The Grande pictured here was the luxury Mustang and came in coupe form only.

the new Mach 1. This came in SportsRoof form only, and with all the appearance cues of a late 1960s sporty car: matt black hood, spoilers, stripes, and racing mirrors. Beneath the skin, there was competition suspension (which was actually the old "heavy duty" option) and a wide choice of V8s (you couldn't have a six-cylinder Mach 1, however nicely you asked): two- or four-barrel 351 Windsor, the 390 or 428 Cobra Jet.

Car and Driver may have loved the Boss 302, but they found the Mach 1 to promise more than it could deliver. The 428-powered car was certainly quick and benefited from Ford's slick C6 automatic transmission, but with that heavy V8 in place, it suffered from terminal understeer.

Above: You could have all these Mach 1 parts with the mid-range 351 Windsor V8, in place of the 390 or 428.

Right: The 351 Windsor was popular choice, in two-barrel or four-barrel form (250 or 290 hp) as in this 1969 coupe with vinyl roof.

Left: For buyers who couldn't afford a Grande or Mach 1, let alone a Boss, there was still the plain and simple Mustang, in coupe, convertible, or SportsRoof form.

Below: This is a 1969 SportsRoof, and in six-cylinder or 302 V8 still offered a sporty looking, relatively economical runabout in the Mustang tradition.

Still, *Car Life* was more impressed with the new Mustang Grande hardtop. Until now, Ford had left the luxury ponycar market to its Mercury division—Mercury's Cougar was based on the Mustang, but with upmarket trim. The Grande sought to emulate that, with a great swathe of extra soundproofing, thick carpets, and fake wood interior trim. Of course, you couldn't have the Grande with spoilers or NASCAR stripes, but *Car Life* thought it made a lot of sense: still reasonably fast and, with the lighter 351 V8 in place, better balanced than the nose-heavy 428 Mach 1. In the years that followed,

Above: In 1969, this was the ultimate Mustang, in horsepower, cubic inches, and E/T—the Boss 429.

Opposite top: The Boss 429 didn't have any of the Mach 1's show-off parts, but then it didn't really need them.

Opposite bottom: Ford only built a few hundred Boss 429s, to qualify the engine (not the car) for NASCAR.

Above: A 1970 Mach 1 351 with all the trimmings. *Motor Trend* tested one against a Boss 302, and found it almost as fast over the quarter-mile, with identical passing times.

Opposite top: The Mach 1 remained the sporty Mustang option through the 1970s, though those downsized ponycars were very different to this one.

Right: No 1970 muscle car was complete without some sort of hood scoop, preferably in matt black, and the bigger the better.

Left: The 1970 Boss 302, aimed squarely at racetrack success to rival the Camaro Z28. Intended for Trans Am, the 302 had a revvy V8 and buckled down suspension.

Below: Ford president Bunkie Knudsen wanted the Boss 302 to be "the best handling street car available on the American market."

upmarket Mustangs would become just as important as the sporty ones.

The Grande made a small but significant contribution to the Mustang's market share, with over 22,000 sold in 1969. Ford also sold over 70,000 Mach 1s, over 60,000 plain SportsRoofs, and close to 130,000 still plainer hardtops. As ever, the bread and butter Mustangs outsold the fancier ones and, even among Mach 1 customers, only a minority (the actual figure was sixteen percent) paid extra for the 428 Cobra Jet. Less than 15,000 convertibles found homes that year, and 3,000 or so Shelby GTs.

Above: For 1970, the ultimate Mach 1 still came with the 428, though traditionally the most popular motor was the basic two-barrel 351—in 1969 only sixteen percent of buyers ordered a 428.

Carroll Shelby incidentally, called a halt to GT production in 1969—he could see that ever tightening safety and emissions legislation was making hot Mustangs a thing of the past.

Overall, Ford sold just over 300,000 Mustangs in the 1969 model year, and despite the formidable competition, it was still the top selling ponycar. This all sounded good, but sales had more than halved since that peak of 1966. In 1970, they slumped to just 190,000. Why? Well, the competition was improving year by year, with the Camaro/Firebird already updated—the new Trans Am variant was a big hit. And the whole muscle car movement

Above: You couldn't miss a Boss 302 (certainly not in bright yellow with black stripes) though it had more serious intent than the Mach 1 did.

Right: Yellow too loud? Orange was one alternative for the 1970 Boss—the last year for the 302, though the name lived on.

Left: *Road Test* magazine headlined its feature on a 428 Mach 1 as the, "Original Ponycar. Fire Breathing Stallion." They definitely liked it.

Below: *Road Test* also predicted that the Mach 1 would become a classic among Mustangs—it typified the muscle car era.

was showing signs of stress. For just a couple of years, it had seemed like there was no limit to power or performance, as manufacturers sought to outdo each other in cubic inches, horsepower, and machismo. Then the accident figures began to come in. Insurance rates rocketed, while the U.S. government began to tighten up on safety and emissions legislation. By early 1970, the golden age of the muscle car was already over, long before the 1973 oil crisis hammered the final nail into the coffin.

Not that you'd know it to look at the Mustang line-up for 1970. The engine line-up was trimmed back to seven, but both the Bosses were still there (though this would be their final year) and *Motorcade* magazine could still write that the Boss 302 was "the closest thing to a sports car

Left: This 1970 SportRoof might look like a Mach 1, but it isn't. The 302 V8 (base Mach 1 motor was the two-barrel 351) gives the game away, as does the lack of front spotlights, another Mach 1 trademark.

Below: A plain 1970 SportsRoof, without the add-on stripes. Even in this form, it's clear that the Mustang had left its compact ponycar roots behind, but an even bigger Mustang was on the way.

Previous page: Even plain SportsRoof Mustangs, like this 1970 example, could be had with the rear spoiler and louver cover.

Ford has ever built in this country." Upgrading from the basic six-cylinder engine to the 300 hp four-barrel 351 cost the customer just $93, so on the face of it performance was still cheap—but that would not be the case for much longer though.

Previous page: Mustang convertibles sold in smaller numbers than either coupes or SportsRoofs, and Ford would stop making them altogether in 1973. In the meantime, this 1970 302 (complete with Shaker hood) offered a last glimpse of carefree fresh-air motoring.

Left: There was no Mach 1 convertible (and needless to say, no Boss either) but the car could be optioned-up with performance parts. This one though, has the mid-range 351 Cleveland V8, with later knock-off wheels.

1971–1973
The Dinosaur

Below: Bigger, fatter, and heavier—the final long-nose Mustang had not worn its years well—seven inches wider and 500 lb. heavier.

Lee Iacocca was not a happy man. He'd finally landed the top job at Ford—Bunkie Knudsen had left—but the Mustang, the car he had nurtured from concept to highly successful reality, had ballooned. Bigger and heavier than ever, it had put on middle-aged spread, and was hardly recognizable as the original "small-sporty." To make matters worse, it was bigger still for 1971, but as Iacocca was the boss, everyone assumed this was his doing.

With hindsight, it's easy to dismiss the 1971–1973 Mustang as a dinosaur, out of tune with its times. Which it was, but for a late 1970 introduction, it was designed and developed in 1968/69, when the muscle car boom was at its height. Ford had previously lost out to their competitors due to a lack of cubic inches in the past, so the 1971 Mustang was designed to take its largest V8s from the start. That's partly why it was nearly seven inches wider and eight inches longer than the original Mustang. It was heavier too—even the basic hardtop now tipped the scales at over 2,900 lb., or 500 lb. heavier than the first Mustang.

The latest Mustang looked big too, especially in SportsRoof form, whose fastback was raked and elongated to resemble that of the Le Mans-winning MkIV. It might have looked good in the studio, but in practice the "bread van rear" (as described by *Car and Driver*) just looked ungainly. And the visibility was terrible; *Car and Driver* complained that "you can hardly see the surrounding earth" and the extreme fourteen-degree rake made the rear

Above: A relatively restrained 1971 Mach 1, showing the radically raked SportsRoof which buyers didn't like.

window almost useless. Customers seemed to agree, and sales of the SportsRoof halved in 1971. The hardtop was, as ever, the most popular Mustang bodystyle, while a mere 6,000-odd buyers chose the convertible. Still, one advantage of the biggest Mustang was that a 429 cu. in.

V8 was a regular production option. But it wasn't the aluminum-headed special of the previous year. The 1971 429 was a destroked version of the big 460 used in Thunderbirds and Lincolns, but on paper at least, it was just as powerful as the previous year's NASCAR special. Ford claimed 370 hp in Cobra Jet form (with or without Ram Air) or 375 hp as a Super Cobra Jet and Dual Ram Air. It wasn't a cheap option—$436 for the Cobra Jet with Ram Air—but that did bring competition suspension as part of the package, plus heavy duty electrics and cooling, a dual exhaust, 3.25:1 rear axle, and (to impress bystanders) a bright engine dress-up kit. The top 375 hp option was clearly intended for drag racers, coming with a compulsory Drag Pak rear axle of 3.91 or 4.11:1.

Right: Mach 1 was still the sporty Mustang, with these plain dish-like wheels as standard, but a Boss had more presence.

Below: The latest Boss
sought to capitalize on the
glamor of the track-bound
cars of the same name.

It all sounded good, but in practice the 429 Mustang
was something of a flop. *Sports Car Graphic* tested the
370 hp version, and found that it was barely faster than a
351, just 0.1 seconds quicker over the quarter-mile. Only

Above: The early 1970s Boss came in 351 or 370 hp 429 form, but road tests found the 351 to be almost as fast, with a 13.8-second standing quarter.

1,250 buyers—less than one percent of the total—paid extra for a 429 in 1971, and the option was dropped before the year was out. The new Boss 351 was probably better value, though this too lost its *raison d'etre* when Ford pulled out of Trans Am racing later in the year. It was usefully more powerful than the Boss 302, with 330 hp and 370 lb. ft.; fast too, rocketing through the quarter in 13.8 seconds. If it guzzled gas at less than 10 mpg, the really committed didn't care, and this latest interpretation of the Boss Mustang handled well too.

Below: The SportRoof fastback, just fourteen degrees from horizontal, looked good but it was impractical on the road—most went for the coupe.

Opposite bottom: All-black vinyl interior was typical of a 1970s performance car, and was roomy for the front two occupants.

Right: The 351 Cleveland V8 proved a worthy successor to the Boss 302, with 330 hp, but emissions legislation would steal its thunder.

But for most buyers, the 302-powered Mach 1 probably made more sense. It still looked the part of a sporty car, with its racing mirrors, color-keyed spoilers, and E70 whitewalls, and *Motor Trend* magazine reckoned that this get-up plus the relatively economical 302, was truest to the original Mustang concept. Incidentally, if you wanted a six-cylinder Mustang, you had to make a point of asking, as the 302 V8 was now the base motor.

Opposite top: Lighter trim colors helped make the most of the SportsRoof's interior, but it was still a dark place in which to sit.

Right: Neat detailing, with the Mach 1 fuel filler cap below the trunk lid lock.

Below: The 1971–1973 Mustang's dimensions are obvious here. The wheelbase was only an inch longer than that of 1964, but massive overhangs accounted for the greater overall length.

Overall, 1971 had not been a happy year for the Mustang (or for any of the muscle/pony cars), but 1972 was worse. Sales slumped to an all-time low of 125,000 as buyers rejected traditional Detroit monsters in favor of more economical imports. And remember those extra factories that Ford turned over to Mustang production, to

Left: Alongside the sporty Mustangs (the Boss and Mach 1 came in SportsRoof form only) Ford carried on the successful Grande. As before, this majored on luxury trim and softer suspension, and only came in coupe form with a vinyl roof. With the 210 hp 302 or 240 hp two-barrel 351 V8, and no performance pretensions, it made for relaxing transport.

Left: The Sprint package was a cosmetic option on SportsRoofs, without going to the expense of a Mach 1 or Boss.

Below: The patriotic red, white, and blue color scheme for the 1972 Olympic Sprint fastback. It also came with white racing mirrors plus color-keyed seats and carpets, low-profile tires, competition suspension, and mag wheels.

Below: You could have a Sprint with color-keyed hub caps and trim rings in place of fancy mag wheels.

keep up with demand? Now the tables had turned, and the Mustang was a one-factory car again. By this time of course, Ford engineers were hard at work on a new generation of compacts, including a Mustang, but that wasn't ready yet.

Left: A shiny 351 Ram Air convertible from 1972, when Ford announced that 1973 would be the open-top Mustang's final year. That decision created a last rush of orders, but in 1971/72 the Mustang convertible sold in relatively small numbers.

Following page: Some thought this 1973 Mustang convertible might be the last new open-top Ford ever. Who would have guessed that a mere ten years later, it would be back with a vengeance.

Opposite and below: 1973 351 Cleveland convertible. Vietnam, Watergate, the energy crisis but, dammit, you could still buy a bright red Mustang convertible.

Below right: Mustangs didn't all come with full instrumentation, but they did make the most of that pony logo.

In the meantime, the old warhorse lost its 429 and Boss 351 options, and for a while the highest powered Mustang mustered just 200 bhp. Things weren't quite as bad as they seemed for hot car nuts, as part of the power drop was due to the stricter SAE (Society of Automotive Engineers) measurement of power. But when the 351 returned mid-year (as the 351 HO) it showed just how hard the manufacturers had to work to keep a performance V8 in the lineup. To clean up the 351's act, it had milder cam timing, a lower 8.8:1 compression, and there were changes to the carburetor and spark advance curve too. Now clean enough to be sold in California, it still produced 275 bhp (SAE, don't forget) at 6,000 rpm, and

Above: Last of the long-nose Mach 1 Mustangs, with repositioned stripes and pegged-back engine options—the top choice was now the 351 Cobra Jet four-barrel, with 248 bhp SAE.

was still a pretty quick car, covering the quarter in 15.1 seconds and reaching 60 mph in 6.6 seconds. And if any private owner wanted to return the 351 to 1971 specifications, that was relatively easy to do, as the 1972 retained its big-valve heads and forged pistons. But really, most of Ford's efforts that year was to clean-up the big-selling Mustang engines (they all acquired evaporative emissions systems) and add new safety features, partly in response to legislation, partly because there was a new public awareness of safety.

As Mustang sales fell to a fraction of those happy hunting ground days, so the lineup shrunk as well. For 1973, the short-lived 351 HO was dropped, and there were now just four engine choices: 250 cu. in. six (80 bhp), 302 cu. in. V8 (140 bhp), and the 351 in 177 bhp two-barrel or 248 bhp four-barrel Cobra Jet form. In the old days, it had been traditional to offer a whole range of rear axle options too, to please drag racers as well as highway cruisers. Now, every combination of engine and axle had to pass emissions legislation before it could be offered, which involved a 50,000-mile test routine. This was obviously prohibitively expensive for the twenty possible

Below: Smaller sales and stricter legislation meant that there were fewer Mustang models to choose from, but the Mach 1 still looked like a true muscle car.

Above: A 1973 351 in suburban setting, where it might still play the role of second/fun car, as Iacocca and the team envisaged.

combinations, so the 1973 Mustang only offered its customers a choice of two rear axles.

Mind you, the Mustang was still available as a convertible, which was a rarity by this time. It was the sole convertible listed by Ford that year, as safety concerns had

Above: Not a Mach 1, but the convertible Mustang could be made to look vaguely like one.

Right: Not an inch of bare metal in sight, but most Mustangs still came with bucket seats, a floor shifter, and three-spoke steering wheel.

seen fewer and fewer buyers opt for an open-top car in the early 1970s. Mustang convertible sales were running at one-tenth the level of those for 1964/65, and Ford finally had to bow to consumer fears and announced that there would be no open top Mustang in 1974. The response was a rush of orders, as buyers sought to snap up what they thought might be the last Ford convertibles ever. Little did they know that the open top Mustang would return ten years later.

Left: A 1973 coupe, and arguably better looking than the SportsRoof, still with that long-hood, short-trunk profile.

Above: The mildly tunneled rear window was a period piece, though also more practical than the radically raked SportsRoof.

Right: A 1973 SportsRoof, with the new impact-absorbing front bumper. This was made of polyurethane on a steel backing, with supplementary rubber shock absorbers. Designed to meet new federal safety legislation, it would return to shape after low speed impacts.

Following page: Nearly 12,000 people ordered a Mustang convertible in 1973, or nearly double the number of 1972. When it was clear the convertible's days were numbered, many bought one while they could.

Above: Those 12,000-odd buyers didn't get a muscle car, but the convertible was still a relaxed cruiser.

Convertible or not, the big, heavy Mustang was no longer a serious performance car. Road tests of the time refer, in lukewarm tones, to "adequate power . . . an amiable vehicle for the freeway." Nice, but no muscle car.

Above: Over ninety percent of buyers chose automatic transmission in 1973; a similar number opted for power steering and nearly eighty percent wanted power brakes. The Mustang was a big car now, that needed power assistance—whatever happened to "small-sporty"?

Exactly the same thing was happening to all its rivals, and GM even considered dropping the Camaro altogether. That was down to new fender legislation, which added yet more weight to the growing Mustang—it now tipped the scales at a hefty 900 lb. heavier than the original "small-sporty." The final long-nose Mustang, in short, was a combination of the worst of both worlds. It had lost its lightweight, compact origins, but its muscular performance (the original justification for making it bigger) had been stripped away too. So less than a decade on from its original rapturous launch, was there still a place in the world for the Mustang?

1974–1979
Un-American Activities

" **T**he Right Car at the Right Time" was how Ford's ad campaign described the all-new Mustang II for 1974, and for once, the hype was true. Just months after the oil crisis hit, in a world of rocketing gas prices and queues at the filling stations, here was a Mustang that could return 23 mpg. It was light and compact, sensible and easy to drive— everything that the 1973 Mustang had not been.

The key to all of this was radical downsizing. The Mustang II was a whole seventeen inches shorter than the car it replaced; it was four inches narrower and weighed 360 lb less. For the first time in a Mustang, there was a four-cylinder engine, the top-power unit was a V6, and there was no V8 option at all. It sounded radical but the Mustang II was really no more than a return to 1964. It was very similar in size to the original ponycar, and aimed to be a sporty-looking but relatively simple and affordable machine. Like that original, it would major on showroom appeal and a long options list to attract the buyers. Maybe all these similarities are hardly surprising—the men in charge of the downsized Mustang were none other than Lee Iacocca and Hal Sperlich, both veterans of the original Fairlane Committee, while styling was overseen by Gene Bordinat and Dave Ash, who had also had a hand in originating the 1964 Mustang.

Launched as a three-door fastback or two-door notchback (no convertible, of course) the Mustang II came with plenty of equipment as standard. There were bucket

Above: You could still buy a Mach 1 in 1974, but it was a very different car to the heavy-metal V8s. Was it trying to be something it could never be? Few testers liked the 2.8 liter V6.

seats, a four-speed floor-shift and tachometer, plus front disc brakes and steel-belted tires. Ford had worked hard to reduce noise, with rubber sheets melted into the floorpan and an isolation subframe. Maybe this was partly why the new Mustang cost several hundred dollars more than the old one: at $3,081, the most basic four-cylinder notchback was just seven dollars cheaper than the 1973 Mach 1 V8!

So not economical to buy, but certainly economical to own, thanks largely to the use of many Pinto parts—Ford's 1970s compact played the same role as the 1960s Falcon had for the first Mustang. The base 2.3 liter four-cylinder engine produced just 88 bhp and 116 lb. ft., though this wasn't far behind the ageing 200 cu. in. six. In any case, the road testers seemed pleasantly surprised by the four. "Much stronger than last year's 2.0 liter and considerably quieter," wrote Jim Brokaw in *Motor Trend*. "The little overhead cammer comes as a surprise," adding that the car, "handles very well, rides better than anything else in its

Below: Whatever you thought of its performance, the Mustang II Mach 1 certainly looked the part inside. The 1975 example pictured here has optional leather interior.

Below: The new Mach 1 came as a three-door hatchback only, with an optional louver cover, just like its predecessor.

class and gives the owner a distinct sense of luxury." Despite the $3,000 price tag, he thought it "a bargain."

The optional 2.8 liter V6 fared less well. Writers thought that it promised more than it could give, and despite the extra cubic inches (or cubic centimetres, as they

Right: Styled wheels and wide tires meant the new Mach 1 could look the part of a sporty car, even if it didn't go like one.

Below: The Mustang II was a better-equipped car than its 1974 predecessor —with fuller trim, full instrumentation, front disc brakes, and plenty of soundproofing.

were now) it lacked torque, and was fussy when worked hard. Only one Mustang II offered the V6 as standard equipment, the Mach 1 fastback, which came with many of the usual sporty car accoutrements—wide wheels, stripes, and black paint—though it was still more restrained than previous Mach 1s. An optional Rally package included stiffer suspension, a limited-slip differential, and dual exhaust. Remembering the success of the Grande hardtop, Ford also offered the Ghia Mustang for 1974, with extra luxury trim and sound system.

This was all very well, but could the American public take a four-cylinder Mustang seriously? The answer was an unqualified yes. Not only that, but they seemed to prefer the four to the V6! During an extended first sales season, almost 386,000 Mustang IIs were sold—not far behind the success of the 1964 original. Only 44,000 of those buyers chose the Mach 1 V6, meaning that most of them weren't looking for a performance car, just an economical, easy to live with, sporty-looking runabout. Ten years on from the original Mustang, history really was repeating itself.

In one way of course, the latest Mustang was different from the old one (apart from the lack of a low sticker price). There was no V8, but a few people knew that in Mexico a Mustang II V8 was already on sale in 1974, a by-product of local content laws. A lot more people knew about it after *Hot Rod* magazine flew south to drive one, and splashed it over their June 1974 issue. After that, Ford U.S.A. had no choice but to press ahead with their own V8 Mustang II. Or maybe they planned it that way all along—who knows?

Whatever the motives, that standard 302 V8 slipped under the Mustang's hood relatively easily, with no major

Above: The Mustang II could have any number of options, including stiffer suspension, limited-slip differential, and dual exhaust on the Mach 1— this is a 1975 example.

surgery, though at first it was only available as an automatic—this was either because the four-speed Mexican Mustang used a different transmission tunnel, or because an American-speed manual Mustang would need recertification, depending on whom you believe. The suspension was beefed up to cope with the heavier motor, which came in detuned two-barrel form, offering 122 bhp

Following page: The Grande was succeeded by the Ghia, which did much the same job of an upmarket Mustang. This 1975 Ghia has the 302 V8, introduced that year.

at 4,000 rpm. Despite which, it was usefully quick, with a 0–60 time of around 10.5 seconds. The keen drivers at *Road & Track* couldn't help pointing out that a European Ford Capri V6 was faster, lighter, and sharper to drive, but then the Mustang was aimed firmly at American buyers.

The heavy V8 also gave the Mustang a frontwards weight bias (60/40, just like that first 390 cu. in. Mustang of 1967) but Ford had worked hard on spring weights and retuning the shocks, and with the Competition suspension package, the V8 handled pretty well. The standard set-up still allowed for a lot of body roll, but it wasn't compulsory. As for the V8, well it was no muscle car, but it boosted the Mustang II from sedan-slow to usefully quick.

Left: Ford couldn't decide whether to offer the new Mustang as a two-door coupe (as here) or three-door hatchback, so they built both.

Above: All of them, from the humblest four-cylinder two-door upwards, had full instrumentation and great attention paid to sound-proofing.

Just to keep that in perspective, the best selling Mustang II in 1975 was the basic four-cylinder notchback, followed by the luxury Ghia. Just over 21,000 buyers chose the Mach 1 (still with a standard V6), accounting for little more than one-tenth of the total. For most Mustang buyers, it seemed, economy was still the watchword, and

Below: The Ghia badge was Ford's attempt to offer some upmarket appeal in the 1970s, and was used on both sides of the Atlantic. Capri—the European Mustang—had its Ghia range-topper too.

Below: The 1978 Ghia
generally outsold the Mach
1 as buyers appeared to
realize that they weren't
getting a performance car,
more of a sporty runabout.

for them, the optional MPG package (with ultra-high 3.18:1 rear axle promising 30 mpg) was probably more significant than any number of V8s.

But everything goes in cycles, and car-buying habits are no exception. In the late 1960s, performance was all, the muscle car boom was at its height. The early 1970s saw a

Below: The 1978 Ghia generally outsold the Mach 1 as buyers appeared to realize that they weren't getting a performance car, more of a sporty runabout.

Below: The power unit for the 1978 Ghia, by which time the choice was between the 2.8 liter V6 or 5.0 liter V8, though neither offered the performance of earlier Mustangs. The basic 2.3 liter four was more popular.

reaction, as buyers sought out economy and sensible transport again, topped off by the 1973 oil crisis. But a couple of years later, things were starting to shift back again. The memory of gas pump queues was fading, and although Americans weren't ready to buy true muscle cars again, they might consider something that looked a little like a hot rod, but still gave good mileage. That was the thinking behind the Mustang Cobra II of 1976.

Or was it? Ford originally intended the Cobra II to be a limited edition special, and farmed out the conversion to Jim Wangers' Motortown concern. They'd reckoned on selling maybe 5,000 of them in the 1976 model year, but

Below: One contemporary observer thought that the Ghia coupe bore a certain resemblance to the Mercedes SL coupe, a comparison that must have delighted Ford.

by August the Cobra II was clearly heading for 20,000. That's when they took it in-house.

Not everyone liked it though. Many castigated the Cobra II as a fake, for beneath the front and rear spoilers, the hood scoop, racing mirrors, and brushed aluminum instrument panel was a standard four-cylinder Mustang. It came in white with blue racing stripes, just like the original

Above: Simple front end treatment for this 1978 Ghia—King Cobra apart, there was little attempt to give the Mustang II an aggressive snout.

Shelby GT 350, and just to underline the association, Carroll himself appeared in the Cobra brochure, giving the car his personal endorsement. If you didn't fancy the white and blue colour scheme, the Cobra II could be had in black and gold, recalling those Hertz Shelbys of the 1960s. "Cobra strikes again . . ." went the brochure, emphasizing that a glorious past had been brought back to life.

Little wonder that some diehard enthusiasts saw this as a cheap betrayal of a hallowed name, but those 20,000 buyers didn't seem to mind too much. *Road Test* magazine tried a Cobra II, and liked it. That was despite being

Above: Woodgrain effect dashboard and trim for the Ghia to underline its luxury pretensions.

Right: Wheels had long been a styling feature of Mustangs, with a variety of options available from straightforward steel to the fully styled, with narrow whitewall tires.

Previous page: Plain and simple silver/blue coupe from 1978, probably with the 2.3 liter four-cylinder engine that most base Mustangs came with.

Below: Spot the Pinto. From some angles, the Mustang II clearly betrayed its compact car origins—many Pinto parts were used under the skin.

Opposite: All Mustang IIs came with a four-speed floor-shift manual as standard, though the later V8 was automatic-only at first.

Right: Some things didn't change. Ten years on from the first Mustang, that galloping pony logo still summed up what the car was supposed to be about.

Below: The King Cobra of 1978. Few buyers were impressed by this ostentatious Mustang II.

humiliated by a genuine GT 350 Mustang in a real-life red-light street race. But as long as there weren't any GT 350s around, the Cobra II was fast enough to be exciting, with a 0–60 mph time of 9.9 seconds, and felt "tight, solid, and

Below: The King Cobra of 1978. Few buyers were impressed by this ostentatious Mustang II.

responsive," behind the wheel. All this and 18.1 mpg. More to the point, *Road Test* found that the look-at-me Mustang attracted more attention than the Ferrari Dino they had on test at the same time. Maybe it was the same old Mustang secret. For most folk, a Ferrari would always be unattainable, but a hot Mustang represented an affordable performance car.

Just a few short years after the convertible was pronounced dead, it was back. Well, sort of. For 1977 Ford announced the new T-top option on the Mustang, which if it wasn't a proper convertible, was at least halfway there. There had been rumors that an all-out

Below: After the success of the Cobra II, Ford pulled out all the stops for the King Cobra. From the deep front spoiler to the alloy wheels, via the giant cobra decal, it did its best, but enthusiasts derided it as a fake muscle car, despite the standard 5.0 liter V8, manual transmission, and competition suspension.

Above: Many King Cobra's left the factory in bright red, but they could also be ordered in black with orange highlights, as here. Either way, no one could misunderstand that here was a car with something to prove.

legislative ban on convertibles was on the way, but the public was already falling out of love with fresh air. Safety concerns (roll over in an open-top car, and the results didn't bear thinking about) were part of the reason, and insurance rates were rising for ragtops, thanks to their vulnerability to vandalism and theft.

But a T-top appeared to offer the best of both worlds. It had been pioneered by the Corvette and Porsche's Targa, and promised most of the fresh air of a full convertible with at least some of the rollover protection of hardtop, with no flimsy ragtop between you and the elements. As fitted to the Mustang II, the T-top consisted of two large tinted glass roof panels. These could be removed altogether, via a single clip on each side, and stowed in the trunk. Wind the windows down, and you could almost be in a proper open-top car, but on cold days fresh air fans could

Below: To modern eyes, the King Cobra looks like a bad case of home customizing gone too far. But it wasn't all fake, as this was the fastest ever factory-built Mustang II.

wind the windows up, turn the heater to max and still enjoy that wind in the hair feeling without freezing to death. To make up for the lack of a rigid roof, Ford strengthened the floorpan and what was left of the roof, but if all this was too radical (or at $600 extra, too expensive) you could also opt for a simpler flip-up sunroof (at $147) or a wind-back one ($243).

Otherwise, 1977 was a quiet year for the Mustang, with very few changes. Unless you count the Ghia Sports and Rally Appearance option packages, both of which majored on appearance items rather than serious hardware. *Motor Trend* tested a T-top Cobra II (the Cobra was back for a second year, thanks to its early success) and praised its steering, handling, and relative economy, while performance was deemed acceptable, though hardly in the muscle car class.

There's a tendency among twenty-first century enthusiasts to dismiss the Mustang II as an unfortunate interlude, and not a real Mustang at all. Yet it kept the Mustang concept alive through some difficult times. Like the original, it was a sporty looking, easy to live with car that didn't cost the earth. And like the original, it sold in droves. In its final year of 1978, the Mustang II was selling better than ever, and over 190,000 went through showroom doors that year. Only one in five of those had the optional V8—1970s Mustang buyers, it seems, had an economy mindset.

But even Mustang II wasn't parsimonious enough for the hard times ahead (as they were seen at the time). The new CAFÉ (Corporate Average Fuel Economy) regulations came into force that year, with an 18 mpg target for all manufacturers' car fleets. Any that didn't would have to

Previous page: Part of the King Cobra package was a T-top, giving at least some of the benefits of a fresh-air convertible.

Below: The 5.0 liter (302 cu. in.) V8 was back, albeit in detuned two-barrel form, offering 122 bhp SAE.

pay a penalty, a gas-guzzler tax. The Mustang II was a compact of sorts, but in V8 form would struggle to meet even that first target, and CAFÉ was due to get tougher, year by year up to a 27.5 mpg standard. In the event, intense lobbying by Detroit softened that to 22.5 mpg, where it stayed for the next twenty years.

So a new Mustang was being developed, lighter and more efficient than the II, but in the meantime, Ford decided to allow its compact ponycar to go out with a decadent flourish. The flamboyant King Cobra sought to

Right: After a few years' absence, the hood scoop was back, though the age of gaping Shakers really was over.

Below: Making the most of the Cobra logo, drawing on a generation's respect for the cars of Carroll Shelby.

recreate the success of the Cobra II, except that it went further. Any color you liked, as long as it was bright red; big color-keyed spoilers and alloy wheels, blacked-out grille, and a giant cobra decal on the hood. And to satisfy those who criticized the Cobra II as being a hollow fake, the King came with the 302 V8

and four-speed manual transmission as standard. There was competition suspension, power brakes and power steering too. *Cars* magazine tested a King Cobra in August 1978, and came away with mixed feelings. At 16.59 seconds over the quarter, this was one of the fastest

Below: Shortly fter Mustang II went on sale, engineers began work on its successor—this Cobra 5.0L was the result.

Left: Mustang II was downsized, but was a simple car based on early 1970s technology. The new Fox Mustang incorporated new thinking.

Below: Two symbols of the pony car, both used to full effect to bolster the Fox Mustang's image: a galloping pony and a cobra, poised to strike.

Mustang IIs of all, and it had flat, stable handling. But the competition suspension gave a ride of vintage-car hardness ("felt as though it was about to fly apart," wrote Don Chaikin), and they didn't like the soft steering, manual gearshift, or its gas guzzling habits. The buying public seemed to agree, and only 4,318 of them actually ticked the King Cobra option box. Maybe the King Cobra really was punching above its weight, but the real story lay with the thousands more buyers who ordered four-cylinder and V6 Mustang IIs—proof that the ponycar concept wasn't dependent on sheer muscle for its appeal.

Top left: With a V8 under the hood, the Fox Mustang would epitomize the reborn muscle car.

Left: Suitably sporty interior for the Cobra V8.

Above: Like the Mustang II, the 1979 Mustang that replaced it came in two-door coupe and three-door hatchback forms.

Following page: This U.K.-registered coupe features the Michelin TRX option, which brought alloy wheels and low-profile tires.

1979–1986
Fox Brings it Home

Below: It was 1979, and a new era for the ponycar, with the lightweight, efficient Fox Mustang. This is an Indy Pace car replica.

Which was the longest-lived Mustang of them all? Certainly not the 1970s Mustang II, which was in production a scant five years. Most folk would choose the original long-nose Mustang, but even that lasted only nine years, and was changed radically in the process. The 1994 Mustang would last for a full decade, but one ponycar beats them all for longevity—the Fox Mustang was on sale from 1979 right up to 1993, almost a decade and a half. In that time, it was transformed from efficient economy coupe and reborn into a muscle car, and without it, the Mustang would not have survived into the twenty-first century.

The Fox Mustang story starts back in the mid-1970s, when it was obvious that any successor to Mustang II would have to be lighter and more fuel-efficient. If the first oil crisis and the CAFÉ fuel consumption regulations suggested that, then the second crisis of 1979 confirmed it.

To design the new Mustang, Ford drew engineers in from Europe—Robert Alexander and Jack Telnack were both Detroit men, but they'd both done design and development jobs across the pond, and brought European engineers back with them. So the Fox had a lot of European thinking. It was based on a shortened Fairmont sedan platform (also the source of that Fox project name) with coil springs all round, and great attention was paid to low weight and aerodynamics.

Above: Those 1979 Indy Pace car replicas had a choice of 2.3 liter turbocharged four or (as here) the 5.0 liter V8, in standard 140 bhp guise.

Opposite top: Details counted on Indy replicas. Being chosen as official pace car was quite an honor and Ford capitalized on it with 10,000 replicas.

Opposite bottom: The galloping ponies reinforced the Fox Mustang's heritage, but mechanically it had nothing in common with the original 1964 car.

They spent 136 hours in the wind tunnel, perfecting the all-new wedge-shape body, and the result was the most "slippery" Mustang yet. It was the lightest too, thanks to pioneering use of plastics, aluminum, and alloy steels. Even the glass was thinner (yet stronger) than before, and at 2,431 lb. the new Mustang was 200 lb. lighter than its predecessor. It was even lighter than the original 1964 ponycar, which when you consider the extra equipment it had to carry (for safety, emissions, and comfort) was a

Left: The T-top (now the "T-Roof") was back for 1982, as customers just weren't satisfied with a conventional sunroof—the T-Roof was a good compromise.

Above: As it turned out, the T-Roof was soon overshadowed by the return of the full convertible Mustang, but it remained a popular option.

genuine achievement. Under the all-new skin though, the power units were carried straight over. Base engine was the familiar "Lima" 2.3 liter four, with the 109 bhp 2.8 liter V6 the next option up. This was actually withdrawn in late 1979, due to supply problems, its place being filled by the same old 200 cu. in. (3.3 liter) straight-six that had powered Mustangs back in 1966. This actually made less

**Below: This is the 1982 GT
Mustang with T-Roof,
though this halfway house
between a convertible and
hardtop was an option on
all Mustangs.**

**Below: This is the 1982 GT
Mustang with T-Roof,
though this halfway house
between a convertible and
hardtop was an option on
all Mustangs.**

power than the 2.3 four, but was a reassuring choice for traditionalists. They would also favor the 5.0 liter V8 (as the 302 was now termed), here in 140 bhp form.

But the really big news was the availability of a turbocharged version of the 2.3 four, offering similar performance to the V8 but with superior fuel economy. With a Garrett AiResearch turbo and two-barrel Holley-Weber carb, this offered 131 bhp in a lighter package and was actually quicker than the V8 up to 55 mph. So Ford was hedging its bets, with a V8 for the traditionalists and a high-tech turbo on hand in case there was another oil shock. The twin strategy seemed to work at first, with 60,000 turbo Mustangs sold in the first year, though reliability problems meant that it had to be withdrawn in 1981—it would later return in 175 bhp form.

Some things hadn't changed though. All the Mustangs had an interior aiming to impress in the showroom, with a full set of instruments, bucket seats, and carpeted panels on the door trims. And of course, there was a whole range of options, including leather trim and a whole list of different sound systems. Buyers could choose between base and Ghia models, in both coupe and three-door fastback body styles (no convertible or even T-top yet) while the Mach 1 was dropped in favor of a Cobra option package, which brought the 2.3 turbo, Michelin TRX tires and alloy wheels, and a suspension to suit. As ever, a stiffer suspension package (now named "Handling") was optional across the range, as were the low-profile Michelins.

The Fox Mustang received a publicity coup early in its career, when it was picked as pace car for the Indianapolis 500. Seen as something of a badge of honor for any American performance car, Ford lost no time in cashing in, building 10,000 replicas. They decided to load all of them with options and charge over $9,000 apiece, but sold them all anyway. The Fox pace replica came with a choice of 2.3 turbo or V8 engines, the Michelin TRX wheels/tires, plus Handling suspension. There was a front spoiler with twin foglights and a full-length power bulge atop the hood. Inside, Recaro reclining seats, tinted sunroof, center console, special sound system and extra sound proofing, plus many other bits and pieces. No color choice though—they all came in pewter metallic, with orange, red, and black striping, though the loud graphics ("Official Pace Car 63rd Annual Indianapolis 500," with a row of galloping ponies) weren't compulsory.

Ten thousand sounds like quite a lot for a limited edition, but then the 1979 Mustang was a very fast-selling car. Just like the 1964 and 1974, it was a hit in its debut year, with almost 370,000 cars sold. That made it the seventh best-selling car in the U.S., grabbing just over four percent of the entire market. As ever, the basic Mustangs were the big sellers, and the most popular power unit was the 2.3 liter four. That economy mindset was still there.

Late in 1979, Ford must have breathed a corporate sigh of relief that it had worked so hard to improve the Mustang's fuel economy. Political turmoil in Iran and OPEC's failure to agree a worldwide price for oil saw gas prices rocket, and the return of those gas station queues. Car buyers either downsized or decided not to buy a new car at all.

Ford's reaction was to downsize the Mustang V8 to 4.2 liters, restrict it with small valves, and add an ultra-high rear axle of 2.26:1. The result certainly drank less gas, but as only 2.7 percent of Mustang buyers actually bought

Below: A 1983 GT with T-Roof, at a time when the 5.0 liter V8 was the only option for the GT.

one the whole exercise was questionable. By contrast, nearly thirty percent plumped for the ageing 3.3 liter straight-six, now with overdrive on its four-speed manual transmission. But the 2.3 liter four was the best engine for

Left: Bring back that fresh air feeling! For 1983, the Mustang convertible was back, despite all those dire predictions of ten years earlier that all open-top cars had had their day. But the fresh-air Mustang would stay with us for the next twenty years, and in the early 1990s, in V8 GT form, typified the Mustang's retro appeal.

these difficult times and two out of every three Mustang buyers in 1980 chose it. Only the turbo seemed to buck the trend, with power up to 150 bhp, though it would be withdrawn later in the 1981 model year.

In fact, with the V8 emasculated, this was now the Mustang performance flag waver, and Ford sought to underline the fact with the McLaren Mustang, one of the first fruits of its new Special Vehicle Operations (SVO) group. The SVO Mustang was a limited production special, with only 250 built for 1980. It looked special too, with a radical bodykit aping the new IMSA racers, and flared wheel arches over wide BBS alloy wheels. The 2.3 turbo was breathed on by McLaren Engines itself, now boosted to 175 bhp, though the price tag of $25,000 ensured that this first SVO Mustang remained a strictly limited edition.

T-top fans had complained that the Fox Mustang offered nothing comparable. There was a conventional sunroof, and something called a "Carriage Roof" (an optional vinyl roof covering, intended to look like a closed convertible!) but neither really fitted the bill. But for 1981 the T-top was back as a fully-fledged Mustang option. Now known as the T-Roof, it was in the same format as previously, with twin glass panels and the same mix of open-top and hardtop advantages. Otherwise, 1981 was an uneventful year for the Mustang, and something of a low ebb from a performance point of view. The SVO Turbo did not reappear, and even the 150 bhp turbo was withdrawn altogether later in the year. You could buy a V8, but still in restricted 4.2 liter form, and in the unlikely event that any V8 buyer still had illusions of performance, it came with an automatic transmission, and nothing else. A five-speed

Below: The GT 350 20th Anniversary Mustang, that pushed Carroll Shelby into taking out a lawsuit against Ford.

manual transmission did join the options list for four-cylinder Mustangs, but purely to provide a high overdrive speed for economical cruising.

But if 1981 was uneventful in the Mustang story, then 1982 more than made up for it. This was the year when

Above: All GT 350 Mustangs were based on the standard GT, but came only in Oxford White with Canyon Red interior trim, and Lear-Siegler articulated sports seats. This one has a non-standard steering wheel—a three-spoke was the original fitment.

Ford's ponycar began its long climb back to real performance. On paper, it didn't look that significant, just the return of the old 5.0 liter V8, with twenty extra horsepower and six percent more torque. But performance figures told a far more spectacular story, and their consequences were far reaching.

As it happened, Ford had to do something—it would surely have known that GM's new generation Camaro and Firebird, announced for 1982, would have a fuel-injected V8 with 165 bhp. With that on the stocks, they simply

Above: All of the Fox Mustangs had the same comprehensive instrument set, but note the 85 mph speedometer, in tune with the 55 mph speed limit then in force across the United States.

Right: Five-speed manual transmission on this GT 350. Early Fox Mustang five-speeds aimed at fuel economy, with an overdrive fifth.

Right: With the 1984 GT 350, Ford was clearly trying to stir memories of the original Shelby Mustang of nineteen years earlier. That too came in white only at first, and even the side decals were in the same style. The 1980s did without Shelby's trademark racing stripes though.

couldn't sit back and expect the 4.2 liter economy-tune ponycar to defend corporate honor. So the full 5.0 liter came back, with a new higher lift camshaft and tougher valve springs—these changes alone made the V8 happy to rev out to 6,000 rpm, whereas before it had been struggling at 4,000. A double-row roller timing chain aided valve control, and there was a slightly larger 356 cfm carburetor.

Below: Ford did have something to celebrate with the Mustang GT, as the performance figures caught up with the muscle car glory days—owners could expect 0–60 mph in seven seconds.

Below: Ford did have something to celebrate with the Mustang GT, as the performance figures caught up with the muscle car glory days—owners could expect 0–60 mph in seven seconds.

That all added up to fourteen percent more power as well as the six percent torque increase, but behind these peak figures was a wider, fatter torque curve, made the most of by a four-speed manual transmission. So when the magazines began to test the new Mustang GT 5.0 in late 1981, they got quite excited. Why? Because here was a Mustang that could accelerate to 60 mph in seven seconds or less, turn in a fifteen to sixteen-second quarter-mile, and top out at 120 mph. *Car and Driver* (not easily impressed) named it "the quickest machine made in America." No doubt about it, the performance Mustang was back.

It was backed up by standard Handling suspension, P185/75R-14 tires on aluminum wheels, a Traction-Lok differential, power brakes, and power steering. The Michelin TRX package was an option. The new GT looked the part too, with body-color front and rear spoilers (which meant red, black, or silver at first) and innumerable details in black: the door handles, wipers, and just about the entire interior. But apart from the new GT look and the rediscovery of performance, there was something else highly significant about the Mustang 5.0, its price. At $8,308, it offered a great deal of performance per dollar, a feature that hadn't been offered to American buyers for over a decade. And although the Camaro wasn't far behind, it would always cost more. In the 1980s, the Mustang would single-handedly recreate the concept of a relatively low-tech, good-value muscle car. Of course, being a Mustang, you could also load it with options and push the price tag up into five figures, but that wasn't compulsory. And as final confirmation that Ford had done the right thing, although Mustang sales fell that year, the proportion of buyers choosing a V8 skyrocketed, from

Right: In its revitalized form, the 5.0 liter V8 would happily rev to 6,000 rpm, thanks to a wilder camshaft and stronger valve springs, so it needed that redline warning.

Below: The Fox Mustang's straight, sharp-edged lines were quite different to those of the Mustang II, and would stay in production for fifteen years.

Right: The GT 350 could be ordered with the same T-Roof option as other Mustangs (though it was also available as a full convertible). The T-Roof continued to offer a good compromise between open-top and hardtop Mustangs, more secure and weatherproof than a ragtop.

three percent to one in four. As the adverts said, "The Boss is Back!"

Meanwhile, life went on for the rest of the range, now reorganized with L, GL, and GLX trim levels, the latter replacing the Ghia. Prices were up all round, and even the four-cylinder coupe L was listed at $6,345, which puts that GT V8 price into its true perspective. In fact, there was an even cheaper way to access that reborn performance. The 5.0 V8 and TRX Handling package could be added to any Mustang as options, which bumped up the price by $1,000. If you could do without the GT's black accessories, that put muscle car performance on the road for less than $7,500—quite a bargain in 1982.

So the 1982 Mustang had reinvented the good-value muscle car. In 1983 it did the same for the convertible.

Left: Around 2,000 of
those 5,000 GT 350s were
built as convertibles, with
a white ragtop to match
the bodywork. Although
the 2.3 liter turbo was an
option, about ninety
percent of GT 350s left the
factory with Ford's 5.0 liter
V8, now offering 175 bhp,
with more to come.

Below: This GT 350 T-Roof also has the TRX option, which combined metric-sized alloy wheels with Michelin low-profile tires, and improved the Mustang's road holding—those wheels looked better than the alternatives too.

Nice though the T-Roof was, it was no substitute for the full open-top that many buyers still yearned for, and in 1983 they got it when the new Mustang convertible was launched in GLX or GT guise, with the full-power 5.0 liter V8 or a new 3.8 liter V6 brought in to replace the ancient straight-six. Both came with a power hood, and the GT added a BorgWarner five-speed transmission, the TRX package, air-conditioning, and power windows among other things. At $13,479, the GT convertible wasn't cheap, and in fact most of buyers went for the cheaper GLX.

There were plenty of them—remember how the Mustang convertible was down to 6,000 sales a year in its final days? The new one scored 23,000 in its first year, so it looked like the buying public were ready for full open-top motoring again.

But a convertible wasn't the only Mustang development for 1983. It was like the 1960s all over again, as a horsepower war developed between Ford and GM, though this time just two models were involved, the Camaro/Firebird, and the Mustang. The Ford ponycar had

Following page: For 1984, the SVO Turbo was back, now with 175 bhp thanks to an air-to-air intercooler. It was about as fast as the V8, with a 134 mph top speed and 0–60 mph in 7.5 seconds, helped along by a BorgWarner T5 five-speed transmission.

lighter weight on its side, so despite slightly less power in 1982 (157 bhp vs. 165) it still had a slight edge in a straight line. But for 1983, Chevrolet launched a 190 bhp version of its fuel injected V8, and Ford had no choice but to respond.

Interestingly, it stuck with a carburetor, bolting a 600 cfm four-barrel Holley on to the V8. A big aluminum air-cleaner and strengthened valvetrain were the only other changes, which boosted power to 175 bhp and torque to 245 lb. ft. No injection or electronic control, just tried and tested means of extracting power from an ageing but simple pushrod V8. In fact, that just about summed up the Mustang of the 1980s. Muscle car it might be, but it began to look increasingly old-fashioned, even crude, against the more sophisticated Camaro. On bumpy corners, the Chevy was well balanced and well controlled, while a Mustang bucked and bounced—the latest Mustang was recreating the muscle car glory days in more ways than one.

Still, that wasn't the only option, and Ford's high-tech alternative was the 2.3 turbo, which returned for 1983, completely redesigned. Bosch fuel injection replaced the carburetor and the motor was strengthened with forged pistons and tougher valves, plus an oil cooler and lighter flywheel. With 145 bhp and 180 lb. ft., the turbo was well short of the revitalized V8, and took nearly ten seconds to reach 60 mph, which was a good three seconds longer than the big-cube motor. It also cost $250 more, so it's hardly surprising that only 500 customers opted to buy one of them in 1983. By contrast, the bigger engines went from strength to strength, and by this time only one in four Mustang buyers were choosing a 2.3 four, whether with a turbo or not.

Who would have thought that Ford and Carroll Shelby would end up in the courtroom? But they did. It was the Mustang's twentieth birthday in 1984, and Ford sought to mark the occasion with a limited edition named GT 350, in memory of the first Shelby Mustang. Based on the GT hatchback or convertible, the 1984 GT 350 came in Oxford White with red trim, a few extras, and an inscribed plaque on the dashboard.

It was a nice idea, but the trouble was, no one had thought to ask Carroll, who was now working for Lee Iaccoca at Chrysler. Shelby was furious, and took Ford to court over unauthorized use of what he thought was his trademark. But he lost the ruling—it was fourteen years since the GT 350 badge had been used, so it was held to be back in the public domain. The twentieth anniversary Mustangs went ahead, and 5,000 were built.

Carroll Shelby might now be in the Chrysler camp, but he appeared to have a successor in terms of special after-market Mustangs. Initially Steve Saleen didn't tune his ponycars, concentrating on aerodynamics and suspension, but quicker than standard Saleen Mustangs did appear later, and these were very much the Shelbys of the 1980s. To this author's knowledge, no American police department in the 1960s ever used Mustangs, but the California Highway Patrol (CHiPS) did in the 1980s. The V8 proved ideal, being relatively cheap, and easily capable of meeting the new CHiPS performance criteria for pursuit cars: 0–100 mph in less than thirty seconds, and up to 120 in less than two minutes.

Meanwhile, Ford persevered with the 2.3 turbo, commissioning the SVO to produce something a bit special. The SVO Turbo Mustang was boosted to 175 bhp,

Below: The 1986 GT 5.0L, with T-Roof, and seven years on from the 1979 Fox Mustang, doesn't appear to have changed very much.

thanks to an air-to-air intercooler, and it was also loaded with every conceivable option with disc brakes all round, Koni adjustable shocks, wide wheels and tires, air conditioning, leather seats, and so on. With all these extras it wasn't cheap either, priced at $15,596 (at $6,000 more than the plain V8 GT model) but the latest upmarket turbo

Following page: The full convertible V8 was rapidly becoming a retro-mobile for 1980s America—there was nothing else like it on the market.

Above: Under the hood, the Mustang GT finally came with electronic fuel injection in 1986, which brought 200 bhp, and boosted peak torque to 285 lb. ft.

proved to be a relative hit, and actually sold 4,500 in its first year of production.

As for the V8 itself, which stuck with its good old-fashioned carburetor (something Ford made a virtue of), but throttle body fuel injection was added to the 3.8 liter V6 (now with 120 bhp and better driveability) and to a new softer version of the 5.0 liter V8. The latter was aimed

Below: This was now the sole performance Mustang, as the 2.3 liter was dropped—for most buyers, only the V8 gave that authentic ponycar experience.

at Mustang cruisers, and produced 165 bhp mated to a standard automatic transmission.

Just a few years previously, it would have seemed impossible. In the 1970s, many people predicted that the age of the muscle car, or indeed any kind of performance car, was gone for good. And convertibles? They were dead too. But move on to the mid 1980s, and the open-top

Mustang wasn't only back, but selling strongly. As for performance, the Mustang V8 had been gaining horsepower by the year. It started out with 140 bhp, then in 1982 the reborn GT made that 157 bhp. For 1983 it was 175 bhp, and would have been 205 the year after, had a last minute technical glitch not held it back. But for 1985, the 200 horsepower Mustang was back—and remember, this was over 200 SAE horsepower, so equivalent to maybe 270–280 hp of the old 1960s sort.

The actual figures were 210 bhp at 4,400 rpm and 265 lb. ft. at 3,400, thanks to a new camshaft, high-capacity stainless steel headers, and low-friction roller

Below: Inviting, isn't it? A Mustang V8 convertible on a sunny day, driver's door open, ready to go. Most of the GTs (as this one) were sold with manual transmission.

Below: Fuel injection for
the GT 5.0L in 1986, but all
other Mustangs (the fours,
V6, and mild V8) had
already taken this route—
Ford managed to make a
virtue out of a necessity
however.

tappets. Carburetion was still courtesy of a four-barrel
Holley (its final year, before electronic injection finally took
over this otherwise low-tech muscle car). But the real
question was could this make it a match for the latest
IROC-Z Camaro? That had more power, but less torque,
and in practice the arch-rivals were very evenly matched,
though the Mustang appeared to have the edge on
acceleration, with a fourteen to fifteen-second quarter
showing up in the road tests, plus 0–60 in six to seven
seconds. In short, the 1985 Mustang GT, relatively quiet
and comfortable, complete with catalyst and capable of
25 mpg cruising on the freeway, was about as fast as the

Below: Fuel injection for
the GT 5.0L in 1986, but all
other Mustangs (the fours,
V6, and mild V8) had
already taken this route—
Ford managed to make a
virtue out of a necessity
however.

original GT 350 Shelby. For keen types, any nostalgia was misplaced, for here in the mid-1980s the muscle car really was back. Just read any road test of the time: there are delighted references to "axle-creaking torque" and "fun." Everyone agreed that the Mustang GT was still a bit rough around the edges, especially when compared to a Camaro, but it certainly wasn't boring.

The cruiser V8 got a power boost that year too, to 180 bhp (mostly due to a larger, less restrictive exhaust) and though the faithful 2.3 liter four was unchanged, it

Below: This is a 1986 SVO Mustang. The SVO Mustangs came in V8 form as the turbo, and with the smoother front end that would appear on all ponycars from 1987, but looked understated compared to the first SVO cars.

was once again the most popular Mustang power unit, making up around half the orders that year. One in three buyers still went for the V8 though. Of course, part of the Mustang's appeal, apart from its low price and stunning performance, was its back to basics specification. That had nothing to do with comfort (inside the ponycar was quite a luxurious beast by the mid-1980s) more with what went on under the hood. By this time, the Mustang was the only serious performance car to still use a carburetor in place of electronic fuel injection. The Camaro had long since gone

the injection route, and Porsche, Mercedes, and Jaguar did too. In fact, by 1986 even the cruising Mustangs—the V6 and milder V8—had followed suit, but the full-power GT stuck with a four-barrel carb.

In terms of muscle car folk-memory, this was highly symbolic. The big four-barrel carb had become a totem of the muscle car era, and nothing worthy of the name was complete without one. To those with long memories (or with nostalgia for a time they were too young to experience first-hand) the four-barrel became even more iconic in later years, when oil crises and emissions concerns combined to make the efficiency of fuel injection an essential on almost every new car. Ford made a virtue of necessity, stressing the simplicity of the Mustang GT against injected rivals, but for 1986 it too bowed to the inevitable, and gave the GT fuel injection.

Injection was a sequential multi-point set-up (the V6 and V8 used a simpler throttle-body type) with electronic control and air density management. Power was actually down slightly to 200 bhp but acceleration times were cut, thanks to a fatter torque curve and a 7.5 percent boost in peak torque to 285 lb. ft. The result was a genuine six-second 0–60 mph time and smoother, easier driving at low speeds. It also made the V8 more efficient, which Ford enhanced with roller tappets, new piston skirts, and low-tension rings, as well as a lower-drag water pump. These all cut friction, giving the V8 a fighting chance of meeting the CAFÉ fuel consumption regulations. With the help of higher gearing, it did so, thus avoiding the gas-guzzler tax and maintaining its status as the affordable muscle car. The new 230 bhp Camaro might have been faster, but it cost hundreds of dollars more, and as for the Porsche 928, that

Below: The last gasp for the Turbo Mustang in 1986, here in 225 bhp SVO guise. Cheap fuel and a changing market brought the big V8 back into favor.

demanded a far fatter bank balance than either. The V8's in-house cousin, the pricey SVO Turbo was dropped—after seven years, Ford finally gave up on its four-cylinder turbo experiment, leaving the V8 as the sole performance Mustang. But losing the turbo didn't hurt sales one bit, which rose by over fifty percent in 1986, to over 244,000, making it the Fox Mustang's best year since its 1979 debut.

1987–1993
Keeping the Faith

Below: The 1987 LX Mustang three-door—the same year of the Fox's only significant facelift.

Ford, it has to be said, got good value out of the Fox Mustang. Not only was it the longest-lived Mustang of them all, in production for fifteen years, but it had no major redesigns in that time. Contrast that with the original ponycar, which was substantially redesigned and rebodied every two years. So Ford didn't spend a fortune on redeveloping the Fox. It was also a relatively simple and cheap car to build, and some major components (notably the four-cylinder and V8 engines) had even been carried over from the 1970s. Maybe it was outdated in some ways, but the Mustang went on selling in big numbers during the 1980s, and it's almost certain that every one of those ponycars made Ford a decent profit.

So that's why Ford made so few changes. There was talk of an all-new car to replace it, and the planned SN8 project looked like the Mustang to do it. Had the SN8 made it to production, it would have marked a radical change in Mustang philosophy, being small and high-tech. This new-generation ponycar was designed to meet the sophisticated European and Japanese coupes head on. Then the Ford bean counters had their say, vetoing what would have been a costly and time consuming car to develop.

Then someone had the bright idea of having Mazda (Ford's Japanese partner) develop a new front-wheel-drive coupe, which could be sold with either Mazda or Mustang badges. Simpler, quicker, and cheaper than going it alone

Above: A new interior featured in the 1987 Mustang, with a more rounded dashboard, minor controls on wing extensions, and a new two-spoke steering wheel.

Left: The name meant so much now that plans for a Japanese-designed replacement caused outcry.

Above: Twenty-five extra horsepower for the 5.0 liter V8 for 1987, as Ford sought to keep up with the Camaro/Firebird. In a straight line, it most certainly did.

Right: A smoother front end identified the 1987 Fox Mustang, reminiscent of the SVO Mustangs.

with the SN8, and in cold business terms a good idea. Until the news leaked out and the ensuing outcry persuaded Ford that maybe a Mustang designed in Japan wasn't such a good idea after all. (This joint project did make it to production though, as the Ford Probe.)

So nothing for it, the Fox Mustang would have to soldier on, though with sales of over 180,000 in 1987, it didn't seem to be doing too badly. A new nose, with a smoother more aerodynamic look, cleaned up the front end, and slimmer C pillars did a similar job at the back, while the GT Mustang got more look-at-me parts, notably a bodykit with front and rear spoilers, sill extensions, and fender trims.

For anyone who thought this was over the top, or who wanted to save $1,500, Ford now offered the full-power 5.0 liter V8 and all the GT chassis parts in the plain LX Mustang. Outwardly, this looked like any other four-cylinder base model, but it performed just like a GT, and was an attractive and good value street sleeper. Of course, customers had been able to order a Mustang like this for years, by ticking the right option boxes, but now it all came together as a package. The LX V8 also weighed 300 lb. less than a GT, so it was better balanced and slightly quicker as well—one magazine claimed a thirteen-second standing quarter, if you fitted a pair of slicks.

Another glossy monthly had speculated that the 1987 model year would see a 250 bhp 351 cu. in. (5.7 liter) Mustang, to counter the threat of the 230 bhp Camaro. That didn't happen, but Ford did boost the standard 5.0 liter up to 225 bhp, the extra power coming from freer-flowing cylinder-heads, a 60 mm throttle body, and a bigger air intake. Incidentally, this was the only V8

Previous page: While most media attention focused on the V8, and ferocious duels between Mustang and Camaro muscle cars, the four-cylinder Fox carried on selling in big numbers. Just like the original Mustang, it offered a sporty looking but economical, affordable package. This is a 1988 three-door automatic.

Left: Ford might not have come up with the 5.7 liter Mustang that some predicted and others longed for, but there were plenty of tuning houses able and willing to do the same job. This 1988 convertible 5.7 is proof of the fact, along with a Shelby-esque paint job.

Above: As the Mustang got older, the attractions of the convertible grew too. The open-top Mustang would soon overtake the two-door coupe in sales.

available now, since the touring option had been dropped the previous year. So to keep cruising customers happy, the full-power V8 was now available with a four-speed automatic transmission as well as the five-speed manual.

Of course, there were always those for whom 225 bhp would never be enough, though Ford showed little signs of

satisfying them in the near future. Mustang never made the suggested 351 cu. in., and a similar fate befell the twin-turbo version, which Ford commissioned tuner Jack Roush to build. Again, there was talk, this time that this 400 bhp range-topper would celebrate the Mustang's twenty-fifth birthday, though it never happened. As a mainstream manufacturer, Ford had to keep an eye on the CAFÉ regulations, on the energy market, and its own public image. The Mustang GT was all very well, but the days of super-wild muscle cars, direct from the factory, seemed to be over.

But if Ford couldn't deliver a super-Mustang, there were plenty of tuning specialists happy to oblige. *Road & Track* took a couple of these hopped-up Mustangs to the Firebird International Raceway in 1988. One was James Bittle's road legal 280 bhp 5.0 liter car, and the other was a

Right: This was the key to that retro open-top experience. Passengers could sit back and hear the V8 burbling away—it was 1966 all over again.

Chris Kaufman offering, though this 5.7 liter Mustang, mustering 330 bhp in Stage 3 tune, was aimed strictly at the track. The Kaufman car rocketed through the standing-quarter in 13.5 seconds, though the Bittle wasn't far behind it at 13.9 seconds. But both cars though, were conclusively smoked by a 500 horsepower nitrous-injected Camaro that *Road & Track* had taken along for the ride.

Most customers didn't need (or simply couldn't afford) this sort of power, and for them the standard Mustang V8's 225 bhp was more than enough, especially as it powered a

Left: GT Mustangs now came with a bodykit as part of the package, which brought front, rear, and side skirts—a fashion of the time, it sought to suggest ground effect aerodynamics.

Above: Anyone who didn't like the add-on bodywork could always opt for an LX Mustang with all the mechanical GT parts, and save $1,500 into the bargain.

Previous page: Steve Saleen built up a strong business out of building converted Mustangs, with Ford's blessing—most were purely road cars.

Right: Racecraft suspension was Saleen's own, with stiffer coil springs, Monroe shocks, special strut mounting bearings, a urethane anti-roll bar pivot, and Saleen's own alignment figures.

Below: Wide wheels and tires were always part of the Saleen package.

Above: In the late 1980s, these two words became strongly linked, just like the Shelby Mustangs of the twenty years earlier.

relatively light, short wheelbase car that could still be a handful to drive hard on twisty roads. Despite its better manners these days, the V8 Mustang could definitely bite back, and it didn't have the user-friendly handling of a modern front-drive coupe. Mind you, some buyers were happy to cruise around in a Mustang that looked as if it

had a whole lot more than 225 bhp. This was where Steve Saleen came in. He was still concentrating on the suspension and body kit parts, leaving engine tuning to others. As a result, Saleen Mustangs of this period were no faster than the standard cars, though they looked more special. Just as much to the point for many buyers, most parts were still covered by the standard Ford warranty, and the cars were sold through Ford dealers. The early Saleen Mustangs were a far cry from those first GT 350 Shelbys.

But 1989 saw a change of heart. The Mustang SSC ("Saleen Super Car") was the first Saleen ponycar with extra power, though whether the claimed thirty percent improvement really existed was a matter for speculation. Saleen claimed that a larger 65 mm throttle body, revised plenum chamber, bigger intake ports, stainless steel headers, and freer-flowing mufflers added up to 292 bhp. *Car and Driver* disagreed. Their test SSC ran through the quarter at 14.2 seconds and to 60 mph in 5.9. It would reach 149 mph in top gear without running out of revs (the SSC was geared high) but *Car and Driver* thought that 292 bhp was a little optimistic—maybe 270.

The SSC was on firmer ground with the chassis, which had always been a Saleen speciality. One of the Fox Mustang's biggest weaknesses, with over 200 bhp on tap, was its flexible bodyshell, and the SSC had substantial braces between the front shock towers and bulkhead, with a similar arrangement at the back. There were Monroe adjustable shocks and Saleen's own stiffer-than-standard springs. Not that this was a stripped-out hot rod—the SSC came with custom-built leather seats and a 120-watt ten-speaker stereo. That partly explained the price tag of $35,000, but then Saleen Mustangs had never been cheap.

By comparison the standard convertible looked like
something of a bargain, at $17,000 in LX V8 guise. It was
more popular than ever, with over 40,000 cars sold in
1989, so much so that Ford dropped the T-Roof option on
hardtop Mustangs. It was easy to see why the open top
Mustang sold so well in the U.S. in the late 1980s. There
was very little else that offered traditional, V8 convertible
motoring at such a relatively low price. Not many people
bought these as day-to-day cars, but loved to have one
sitting in the garage, waiting for a sunny Sunday. As an
affordable fun car, this latest fresh-air Mustang had much
in common with the 1964 original.

You didn't need to be a mathematician to work out
that this made 1989 the car's twenty-fifth anniversary, not
that you would have known it from Ford's low-key
response. Small commemorative plaques were screwed to
the dashboard from April 1989 onwards (exactly a
quarter-century since the original launch) but that was
about it. For reasons best known to its corporate self, Ford
chose not to celebrate the Mustang's twenty-fifth birthday.
Maybe Carroll Shelby's reaction to that twentieth
anniversary convertible put them off.

Some said that Ford's special edition convertible for
1990 was its real birthday Mustang, and the brochure that
year did include a fleeting reference to the fact that
Mustangs had been around for twenty-five years. Others
maintained that the convertible was part of a 7-Up drinks'
promotion, and pointed out that its twenty-fifth
anniversary dash plaque had been fitted to all production
line Mustangs since April 1989. Either way, it was based
on a 5.0 liter LX open top, in special Deep Emerald Jewel
Green, with a white leather interior and matching white

Left: Air-conditioning and in-car entertainment were desirable items.

Below: Ford's 5.0 liter V8 underpinned the Mustang's muscle car revival.

Following page: The 1989 GT 5.0L convertible had much in common with a 1932 Ford V8 convertible. Both were relatively cheap, high performance Fords, with less than sophisticated suspension.

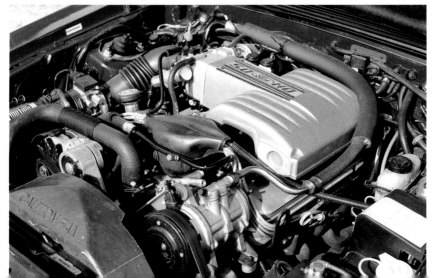

ragtop. There were GT-style turbine alloy wheels, and a luggage rack on the trunk. All but ten percent of these convertibles (Ford built 4,301 of them) came as automatics, underlining the fact that open-top Mustangs were often chosen by more laid back drivers.

They were certainly getting a traditional package. In *Road & Track*, Dean Batchelor compared the bright red convertible he had on test with his own 1932 V8 Ford Roadster. Both were one of the fastest cars available at the time, both were good value compared to the competition, and both had live axles that could be upset on bumpy bends. More than ever, the Mustang convertible was being referred to as a "retro" car. It never set out to ape a 1960s style from the drawing board, that's just the way it was.

Not that everyone went for the traditional V8 option. We often associate the four-cylinder Mustang with the crisis-ridden 1970s, but despite the V8 revival, it remained a popular option through the 1980s as well. At one point, sixty-two percent of Mustang buyers were choosing the quiet, economical four in preference to the V8. So while the full-power convertible seemed like a throwback to the 1960s, the 2.3 liter four kept the faith with another facet of the original Mustang: it was a relatively small, economical car with sporty looks and a low-ish price tag. And in 1990, despite a near-$10,000 sticker price on the base Mustang, that's what it was.

For 1991, the cheapest Mustang actually cost $10,157, but it was still a good-value coupe, especially in V8 form. Upgrading to the 225 bhp V8 added $3,000 to the price, but gave access to near-supercar acceleration for around $13,000. Despite twenty-five years of price rises, a V8 Mustang was still a performance bargain. Not that

Below: Featured here is a 1989 LX 5.0L three-door. This particular car has a GT-style front spoiler and spotlights, but both in standard form.

everyone was impressed, and Fox Mustang sales actually slumped to a new low in 1991, to just fewer than 99,000. This was actually the Mustang's worst annual figure ever, and could only be partly explained by a general decline in American car sales.

Still, there were a few improvements for 1991, though the Fox Mustang would see no big changes in the last few years of its life—it would be replaced for 1994 by an all-

new fourth generation ponycar. The V8 engine remained, in its 225 bhp/300 lb. ft. form, though the 2.3 four was updated with twin-plug ignition. Having two plugs per cylinder gave more complete combustion, cutting emissions and boosting power to 105 bhp (a seventeen percent increase). It could also manage 30 mpg on the highway, according to official figures, so a four-cylinder Mustang was nearly as fuel-efficient as a Japanese coupe. There were

Below right: The LX made a mild looking, but very fast, street sleeper, as well as being slightly quicker than the heavier GT.

new five-spoke alloy wheels as well, with 225/55ZR-16 tires to suit.

All very worthy, but not exactly the stuff of which exciting road tests are made, though the magazines didn't neglect the Mustang, as there were plenty of tuned versions

Above: Saleen finally launched a tuned Mustang in 1989. The SSC claimed 292 bhp, though 270 was probably nearer the mark.

to keep the pages filled. Perhaps the most radical of these was the Cartech turbocharged Mustang, with a claimed 392 bhp at 5,000 rpm and 550 lb. ft. at 4,200. Tuners often over-stated the effect of their work, but 0–100 mph in eleven seconds (plus 0–60 in 4.9) appeared to back up Cartech's claims, especially as those times were taken with a high 2.73:1 rear axle. Perhaps even more impressive was that the whole package was street legal, and included catalytic converters. As for top speed, Cartech boss Corky Bell was convinced he could make this the first ever 200 mph Mustang. He did it too, though the record car was very special, with eight Haltech fuel injectors and 15 psi of turbo boost. At Fort Stockton in Texas, mustering a claimed 371 hp at the rear wheels, the ultra-special Cartech Mustang was timed at 203 mph.

A lot of people liked to read about Mustangs like that one—some folk might even go as far as buying one—but all the excitement of these hot rod Mustangs masked a simple unpalatable fact: the car itself was losing its legendary popularity. In the early 1990s, sales slid as the Mustang's age began to put buyers off. Nineteen-ninety one was the worst year yet . . . until 1992, when sales dipped below 80,000 for the first time.

It wasn't just that the Fox Mustang was an old car. It was also an open secret that a new Mustang was only a couple of years away, and nothing is more damaging to sales of an old car than the expectation of a new one just around the corner. In fact, more buyers than ever seemed to be choosing a Mustang as a sort of retro experience, which meant more were opting for a convertible. The practical three-door hatchback remained the most popular choice, but in 1992, open-top sales overtook those of the notchback coupe for the first time. That doesn't mean to say that all those customers were buying V8s—sales were split roughly 50/50 between the V8 and twin-plug four. Ford had wisely kept the little 2.3 on board even at the height of the V8 boom, and for thousands of buyers, a four-cylinder Mustang made a pleasant alternative to an imported coupe.

There would never be another Shelby Mustang (though that's probably a rash prediction) but in 1992 the Shelby Automobile Club did commemorate the original with their own special Mustang. The idea was for a limited edition that would evoke memories of the first GT 350, and being offered to faithful SAAC members, it would be sure to sell in limited numbers. Best of all, Carroll Shelby gave the

Below: A 1992 GT, as it left the factory. By now, Fox Mustang sales were finally on the slide, as most folk knew that a new Mustang was imminent.

project his blessing (after all, this wasn't Ford the corporation cashing in on his heritage) and the Shelby AAC Mk1 Mustang went into production. Just like the original, it used standard tuning techniques to squeeze out more power, plus stiffened-up suspension and uprated brakes. *Motor Trend* magazine thought the result was great fun in short doses, just like the first GT 350, but that it

Below: The 1993 SL GT with chrome alloys, extended rear spoiler, and the usual bodykit parts. It had come a long way since the original fuel-efficient coupe, of the 1970s.

was also noisy, bumpy, and a little too close to the action to use as an everyday car. Sounds just like the original.

If 1992 was Fox Mustang's slowest-selling year, then 1993 was its most challenging. Not only was the new Mustang just a few months away, but the F-body Camaro and Firebird had been launched, making the Mustang look more like a hotted-up hatchback next to a real sports car. However, Ford did have a final couple of weapons in the Fox Mustang armory.

First and biggest news was the Mustang Cobra. This was a no stripes and paint special like the 1970s cars, but a thoroughly reworked machine, first fruit of the new SVT (Special Vehicle Team) and SVE (Special Vehicle Engineering) groups. These replaced SVO, but their job was much the same, to produce limited edition hot Fords based on production cars.

So the Mustang Cobra boasted 235 bhp from its upgraded V8 (Ford now quoted just 205 bhp for the standard Mustang, for no apparent reason): GT-40 cylinder heads with bigger ports and valves were the main changes, plus a new cam and larger 70 mm throttle body. The five-speed manual transmission (the same Borg Warner T5 that had served so long and so well) was uprated too, there were ventilated disc brakes all round plus low-profile tires on seven-inch wide alloy wheels. As for the suspension, this was carefully set up with relatively soft springs and competent damping, aiming to provide a good ride as well as handling.

Car and Driver pitted a Cobra against the latest Camaro and Firebird, and they reckoned that Ford's specialist divisions had done a good job of improving a basically outdated car. But it was not enough of an

Above: A 1993 SL limited edition convertible, built to boost interest in the old Mustang in its run-out months.

improvement to beat the competition, which were better handling cars (despite its more sophisticated suspension than previous hot Mustangs, the Cobra could still bite back) and more competent all round. They also offered up to 275 bhp, which made even the Cobra look a little lacking in venom.

Still, the Cobra fulfilled its job of renewing customer interest in the Mustang, as did a couple of limited edition convertibles in this farewell year for the Fox. Offered in either Canary Yellow Clearcoat or Oxford White, these had various body color parts and a galloping pony logo embossed on to the headrests and floor mats (remember that option from 1966?). The white car came with complementary white interior and white alloy wheels, while the Canary had chrome alloys plus a white or black interior. About 1,500 of each were built. The Cobra and those convertibles did their job, and sales actually recovered in 1993, but everyone knew that these were Ford's way of saying farewell to the long-serving Fox. The big news—the first new Mustang for fifteen years—was about to arrive.

Right: A body color spoiler, mirrors, and trunk hinges were part of the package, along with a black or white interior. And with that, it was farewell to Fox.

1994–1998
Curves are Back

Below: The fourth-
generation—thirty years on
but still with a cast-iron
pushrod V8 driving the rear
wheels via a live axle.

Below: The fourth-generation—thirty years on but still with a cast-iron pushrod V8 driving the rear wheels via a live axle.

T
he fourth generation Mustang was launched for the 1994 model year, and looked quite different from the Fox, but underneath its shapely new bodywork, some parts were the same. In fact, there were 500 of them, including a shortened Fox platform, though Ford were at pains to point out that most of those 500 were parts that didn't affect performance. Still, a glance at the spec sheet revealed how similar Fox and Fox-4 (the "4" for its introduction year) were. Both used MacPherson strut front suspension, a live rear axle, and rack and pinion steering, with a cast-iron pushrod V8 (the very same cast-iron V8) providing the motive power. No wonder that early prototype Fox-4 components were bolted into a standard Fox for road testing.

None of which really mattered. The Fox-4 design team had been instructed to give the new Mustang a better ride, handling, and steering than the old one. It had to be faster, have better brakes, climate control, be quieter and more comfortable, and, of course, it had to look like a product of the 1990s. That they did all of this, based on the same basic mechanical layout, was something of an achievement. The clever point about the styling was that the new curvaceous Mustang looked every inch the sporty coupe, yet it was still a useable four-seater, unlike the lower, less practical F-body Camaro, which had gone further down the sports car route. No hatchback this time, but the Fox-4

was designed from the start to come as a convertible, so
extra strength was designed into the bodyshell—if the old
Fox had a fault, it was in its flexible body, but the Fox-4's
was far stiffer.

The four-cylinder option was dropped (one reason why
the new Mustang never matched the best sales of the old

Below: The new bodyshell was a lot stiffer and less flexible than the old Fox—it had been designed from the outset as a convertible as well as a coupe.

one) and in its place came a 3.8 liter V6. This well proven unit offered a lot more power (145 bhp) and torque than the old 2.3 four, but in practice was little faster, partly thanks to very high gearing to maximize its CAFÉ figures, and partly because the new Mustang was 300 lb. heavier than the old one—the stronger, stiffer body, not to mention

Above: Now with 215 bhp, the cast-iron 5.0 liter V8 was starting to look a little inadequate against a 275 bhp Camaro. The Mustang had weight on its side, but that wasn't enough.

Opposite: The Mustang went all curvy in 1994, but they soon dated, forcing Ford to give the Mustang a more aggressive look.

impact side protection and dual airbags, all added poundage.

So, it was sleeker, stronger, but not radically different to the old Mustang, and the 1994 car also represented value for money, despite the loss of a four-cylinder lead-in model. The base V6 coupe (the LX tag had been dropped) started at $13,355, with a V8 GT convertible costing $21,960. That made it on par with quite ordinary Japanese-built coupes such as the Toyota Celica and Honda Prelude—thirty years of heritage came as standard.

But the crucial question was how did it measure up to the Camaro, which appeared much more of a serious sports car? On paper, it didn't look good, with the ageing

Mustang V8 motor offering 215 bhp in its latest guise—the Z28 Camaro countered with 275 bhp and 325 lb. ft. There were lower-powered Camaros too, but the top-line Z28 was closest to the GT on price. So not surprisingly, it was far quicker. *Car and Driver* placed the two side by side on the drag strip, and did the business: a 14.1-second quarter-mile and 5.4-second 0–60 time for the Camaro, but the Mustang lagged with 14.9 and 6.1 seconds respectively. In fact, the GM ponycar also scored higher in its engine, brakes, handling, value, styling, and even on driving fun. And the Mustang? Well, the testers thought it felt far superior to the Fox, and with better comfort, ride, and practicality than the latest Camaro. But that didn't make it a muscle car.

Ford promised that help was on the way, in the form of its new-generation 4.6 liter V8, which was already seeing service in other cars. But it wouldn't be available in the Mustang for a couple of years, and in the meantime SVT came up with a new Cobra to at least partially help to fill the gap. The faithful 5.0 liter V8 was boosted to 240 bhp at 4,800 rpm while the Cobra weighed around 100 lb. less than a Camaro Z28. It also maintained SVT's compliant suspension philosophy (softish springs with good damping) plus bigger brakes with ABS, wider wheels, and low profile tires. It was also picked as the pace car for the Indianapolis 500, the third time a Mustang had been chosen. As before, Ford made the most of this publicity coup by offering pace car replicas. One thousand of these were built, all of them Rio Red convertibles. They didn't have the genuine pace cars' fifteen-gallon fuel tank and stiffer rear springs, but did come with a saddle-leather interior and ragtop.

Previous page: The GT from 1995, the final year for the 5.0 liter V8—Ford urgently needed to give the Mustang an engine bay boost.

Meanwhile, the gap between the base V6 Mustangs and the V8 GTs was filled by the GTS, a slightly cheaper version of the standard GT. This did without the sports seats, foglights, and rear spoiler, but was otherwise identical to the GT, except for saving $1,000 on the price. It really did the job of the old LX 5.0 liter, which also

offered GT performance with fewer trimmings. Another
new feature for 1996—an optional hardtop for the
Mustang convertible—was less successful. Heavy and fully
trimmed (complete with interior light) this was intended to
be a winter-long fitment, which the convertible owner
would bolt on to the car in the fall and remove it again

Above: 1996 Cobra SVT
Chameleon with that
handbuilt DOHC 4.6 liter V8
that proved so popular,
though not without its
own problems at first.

(with the help of a strong friend) come spring. Only 500 were sold.

None of these really addressed the Mustang's basic performance shortfall compared to a Z28 Camaro, but the answer (for buyers with thick enough wallets) was the latest Saleen. Steve Saleen had lost no time in modifying the new Mustang, and for around $35,000, buyers could have a Saleen S-351 Mustang sitting in the driveway. Based on the standard car, this was fitted with Ford's 5.7 liter Windsor V8; tuned with a new cam, bigger throttle body, bigger valves, and different engine management. The result, claimed Saleen, was 371 bhp, and if that was true then the Camaro Z28 had met its match—at a price.

Steve Saleen wasn't alone in offering a 5.7 liter Mustang, and Ford itself did too, albeit via SVT and in a strictly limited edition run of 250. This was the Cobra R, which didn't use the Windsor V8, but instead sourced a cylinder block from a Ford marine motor, and added aluminum alloy pistons, GT-40 heads, a new cam, and stronger internals. That made 300 bhp and a very strong 365 lb. ft., but the Cobra R wasn't intended as a day-to-day road car. SVT sold it with no air-conditioning or radio, and even some of the soundproofing was removed, so it was clear that the R was destined for track use only. All 250 of them were pre-sold.

Meanwhile, the standard production Mustang finally got its heart transplant for 1996. The trouble was, this long-awaited performance transformation didn't look too hopeful on paper. The 4.6 liter V8 had overhead cams, but only one per bank. There were just two valves per cylinder and the block was of cast-iron, so anyone expecting an exotic new alloy V8 would have been sorely disappointed.

Below: 1996, and the 1990s Mustang finally got its new plant, in the form of Ford's modular 4.6 liter V8, here in basic single overhead, two-valve guise in this GT convertible.

Ford was careful to claim the same power for the 4.6 as for the outgoing 5.0—215 bhp and 285 lb. ft. So no great leap forward, but a closer look at the 4.6 revealed plenty of potential for tuning, as it had a lot of in-built strength, and the overhead cams promised a higher rev ceiling.

Sure enough, the SVT Cobra launched alongside made the most of that potential. Here was the new Mustang V8

Following page: Even in latest 4.6 liter form, the Mustang still didn't have Camaro-crushing ability. But the new 4.6 had great tuning potential, as shown in the 305 bhp Cobra.

that some had been hoping for all along, with an aluminum block, four valves per cylinder, and twin overhead cams per bank. It was quite a special piece of kit. The cylinder block was cast in Italy, and the cast-iron crank was German. Everything was shipped to Ford's plant in Romeo, Michigan, where a dedicated team of twenty-four (in twelve teams of two) would carefully assemble this DOHC thirty-two-valve V8 by hand. To emphasize the Cobra V8's hand built nature, Ford had each pair of engine builders sign their names on a plate on the cam cover. It was a technically advanced engine too, with twin 57 mm throttle bodies, an 80 mm air mass sensor, and a butterfly valve in each secondary intake tract. Closed at low revs, this diverted the intake charge through the primary tract only, increasing air velocity (and thus mixing and burning) but at 3,250 rpm it opened up, allowing twin-track intakes for maximum volume and air flow.

All this exotic hyperbole was backed up by figures, with Ford claiming 305 bhp for the Cobra, and 300 lb. ft. at 4,800 rpm. It revved harder than the two-valve V8 as well, with a fuel cut-off at 6,800 rpm. Not that the new car was without its problems. Early examples overheated on hot days, until Ford issued a cooling upgrade kit, and the new BorgWarner T-45 transmission bent its shifter forks. The V8's accessory drivebelt could squeal alarmingly, and even jump off its pulleys. Despite which (and a price of over $27,000 for the convertible Cobra) this was the most popular SVT Cobra yet, with over 10,000 sold.

Road & Track tested one, and thought that the twin-track intake offered the best of both worlds, with a zest for high revs not seen in a production Mustang V8 for many years, plus low rev torque. But they also maintained that

Left: Steve Saleen was quick to turn his attention to the new Mustang, as this 1997 convertible shows. By that time, he was making modest changes to the 4.6 liter V8, but only enough to claim an extra five horsepower.

Below: Saleen S-281 Mustangs came based on the standard GT (220 bhp) or Cobra (310 bhp), but the ultimate was the supercharged S-351, with six-speed manual transmission—this is one of those.

the bottom end delivery was still a little soft, and pointed out that the Cobra made only 15 lb. ft. more torque at peak than the standard Mustang.

But their most surprising conclusion was that despite the European-style bodywork, despite the exotic alloy V8, and all the hard work put into making this a comfortable, quiet and convenient Mustang, this was still quintessentially a product of Detroit. It was, "as American as a John Wayne film festival," faster than many European

sports cars from a standing start, and cheaper than any of them. Not that it could corner with the same aplomb, and *Road & Track* found that even this fourth-generation Mustang still flexed and twisted when driven hard round bumpy corners. That was in open top form of course—the coupe was stronger all round.

Still, the new Mustang had retained its made-in-America feel, finally had a new engine to do it justice, and

Above: A supercharger was standard on the S351, mated to a 5.7 liter V8, making this probably the fastest Mustang available.

Opposite: Curvy interior to suit a curvy car, and more cossetting than the straight-edge dashboard in Fox Mustang.

Right: All Fox-4 Mustangs had this air intake, just in front of the rear wheels.

326 The Pocket Book of the Mustang

all was right with the world. Or was it? While the Cobra strode ahead, standard Mustang sales were falling. From a high of 185,000 in 1995, they slumped to just 108,000 by 1997. GT sales suffered especially badly (maybe some of those GT buyers were ordering Cobras instead) with sales halving between 1996 and 1997. The best selling Mustang was the cheapest one, the V6 coupe, now with 150 bhp.

There's often a difference between magazine reports on cars and their popularity with the public, a point underlined by the fortunes of the 1998 Mustang. Read the road tests, and it looked like a no-hoper against the Camaro, yet sales bounced right back up to 175,000, while

Above: Wide wheels and low-profile rubber looked the part, but *Road & Track* thought the Camaro cornered better than the Mustang Cobra.

Right: A 1997 SVT Cobra packing 305 bhp, the same as the Camaro Z28, but fewer cubic inches meant less torque—a Z28 was quicker over the quarter-mile.

Above: This wasn't the view that Camaro drivers had of a Mustang very often. The Mustang lagged behind on acceleration and understeered around corners.

Chevrolet was considering dropping the Camaro, because it was selling so slowly. On paper, a Z28 Camaro and Mustang Cobra looked just about even, with both offering the customer 305 bhp. The Mustang was 100 lb. lighter, but the Camaro offered an extra 35 lb. ft., peaking at 800 rpm lower down the range. In practice (or at least, in the practice of road test acceleration tests) that torque advantage proved decisive. The Chevy was faster over both the quarter-mile (by 0.3 seconds) and to 60 mph (13.9 seconds and 5.4 seconds respectively), and felt faster as well, according to writer Kim Reynolds of *Road & Track*. The Camaro might not have thirty-two valves and DOHC, but its pushrod V8 was a highly developed, well-proven unit straight out of the Corvette, both torquey and revvy. Nor was it just about acceleration. According to *Road & Track*, the Camaro went round corners better than the Mustang ("a hopeless understeerer") and was nearly $5,000 cheaper—a Mustang GT beat it on price, but of course that was way behind on performance. But despite all of that, Kim Reynolds ended up handing victory to the Mustang. He had more fun driving it, finding it nimble and entertaining, whereas the Camaro was maybe a bit too much of a serious sports car.

Below: The SVT Cobra's DOHC V8 in all its 32-valve, autographed cam cover glory. It revved hard and made a lot of power, though its lack of cubic inches showed against the 5.7 liter Camaro.

The bottom line was that the Mustang was now outselling both the Camaro and Firebird combined, and still retained all of those key ponycar virtues. If you avoided the Cobra, it was still a good-value car. Maybe it didn't have class-leading performance any more, but it looked terrific, and the standard GT did finally get that

much needed power boost for 1998, to 225 bhp. In any case, most buyers were happy to admire those looks and choose from a long list of options in the showroom. Sounds familiar? Well, Mustangs had always been about looking good and impressing in the dealer's showroom, so some things hadn't changed.

Below: The GT lagged behind a Z28 in the performance stakes, though it was cheaper and some thought more fun.

1999–2004
Faster & Sharper

Below: Five years on, the Fox-4 Mustang got a face-lift: New Edge styling, more power, and independent rear suspension.

Dynamically, three things held back the mid-1990s Mustang: compared to the Camaro, it still lacked power; the live rear axle could still make life exciting on bumpy bends; and not everyone liked the curvy styling. For 1999, all three problems were addressed. First off, there was more power right across the range. The V6 offered 190 bhp (up by twenty-five percent) thanks to improved airflow in the heads, a new intake manifold, and low-friction pistons. The V8's airflow improved too, along with bigger valves, a higher lift cam, and other changes, enough to take power up to 260 bhp at 5,250 rpm and 300 lb. ft. Meanwhile, over at SVT, the Cobra DOHC V8 now produced a whole 320 bhp and 317 lb. ft.

All this extra power would have been pointless without the underpinnings to back it up, and the Cobra had them. Back in 1964, some folk had been disappointed that the Mustang carried an ordinary live rear axle and leaf springs, but Ford promised that a genuine, fully independent system was on the way. Thirty-five years later, the SVT Cobra finally delivered. It used an aluminum differential case from the Lincoln Mark VIII, with upper and lower control arms attached to a welded tubular subframe; and all four mounting points were unchanged, so the system could theoretically be fitted to any modern Mustang. The benefits were huge, including a dramatic reduction (125 lb.) in unsprung weight as well as improved suspension control.

As icing on the cake, TCS (traction control system) was now an option on all Mustangs, using the ABS hardware to minimize wheelspin.

Road & Track were duly impressed when they put the latest spec Cobra up against a Camaro SS. For the first

time, here was a hot Mustang that showed true handling sophistication. It would move from mild understeer to controllable oversteer on demand, aided by revised steering, and no longer lost its cool over mid-corner bumps. The new set-up even managed to provide a decent

Left: 1999 was the Mustang's thirty-fifth anniversary, and Ford celebrated by building 5,000 Limited Edition GTs, (coupes and convertibles). This open-top is in Performance Red, but there were other colors to choose from.

Below: Ford appeared to have learned that milestone anniversaries were well worth celebrating, and both 35th and 40th birthdays would be marked with special editions, and helped sell cars. Who knows how they'll celebrate the Mustang's half-century?

Above and opposite top: Given the success of the 1980s Mustang convertible, there was no doubt that the 1990s version would come in ragtop form too—fresh air was still part of the Mustang experience.

Opposite bottom: For 1999, all Mustangs offered more power, with even the base 3.8 liter V6 mustering 190 bhp. Standard GT V8s like this one were up to 260 bhp, with 320 bhp for the SVT Cobra.

Following page: Just look at those creases, sharp enough to cut yourself on. New Edge styling transformed the look of the Mustang, making the most of light and shade to emphasize its shape.

ride as well. In short, the Mustang had been transformed from a rough road car, difficult to control on the edge, into a smooth and sophisticated performer. In Cobra form, it was even closing the acceleration gap with the torquey Camaro as well.

It was closing the styling gap too. The curvaceous 1994 Mustang certainly looked more special than the boxy Fox, but some thought it a little too rounded for its own good, even bland. Next to the F-body Camaro, all straight edges and sports car attitude, it looked like a cosmetic coupe, less of a serious performance car. So for 1999 it had a thorough face-lift with what Ford called New Edge styling: sharper edges and creases gave it greater presence, and a larger front grille (with a prominent galloping pony emblem) had a more aggressive look. And finally, as this was the Mustang's thirty-fifth anniversary (and Ford

Above: Not everyone could afford an ultimate Saleen S-351, but Saleen's "standard" offering was the S-281, using the 4.6 liter V8 in standard or Cobra form. This is a convertible Speed model.

Opposite: If a Saleen was too look-at-me, then the standard coupe, looked cool and classy, and clearly a four-seat coupe, not a sports car like the Camaro.

appeared to have learnt that such milestones were well worth celebrating) there were 5,000 Limited Edition GTs to mark the occasion, in Black, Silver, Crystal White, or Performance Red.

There were very few changes to the basic Mustang for 2000, just the addition of child seat anchor brackets to the rear seats, three new colors, and a new glow-in-the-dark internal trunk release (to reassure nervous owners, fearful of car jacking incidents which might see them bundled into their own trunk). But the Mustang got plenty of public attention that year, albeit of the wrong sort.

The 1999 Cobra, which had so impressed all the magazine testers with its newfound power, its independent rear suspension, and New Edge styling, was the subject of a total recall. Why? Well it seemed that many of those

Above: The specially-made 5.4 liter DOHC V8 made a claimed 385 bhp and 385 lb. ft., but just 300 were assembled in the Cobra R for 2000.

Left: A true limited edition, the 2000 Cobra R was something to be cheerful about while all the 1999 Cobras were being recalled.

Opposite: One thing was certain, the Cobra R certainly turned heads.

Left: It might look like an ultra-fast road car, but the Cobra R was really equipped for the race track, with a Tremec six-speed transmission, aluminum driveshaft, and 3.55:1 rear axle. There were Brembo disc brakes all round, Bilstein shocks, and Eibach springs—in other words, some of the best ancillary components available. It was still overgeared, but would reach 170 mph in fifth gear and, despite the tall overall gearing, could cover the quarter-mile in 13.2 seconds—quicker than any Mustang of the classic muscle car era.

Below: Read the registration plate—"retro" is right, but now this came from badging and image (instead of an ageing technical specification) plus ABS, traction control, and electronic fuel injection.

Opposite bottom: Somebody has a sense of humor, though twin throttle bodies and a free-flowing exhaust gave the Bullitt a usefully fatter torque curve than the standard GT.

Right: Special alloys were part of the Bullitt package, and of course, the car was exactly the same shade of Forest Green as the 1968 Mustang fastback driven by Frank Bullitt, San Fran detective.

Cobras weren't making their claimed 320 bhp, and it turned out to be a fundamental design fault. Late in the design process, the exhaust system was squeezed, to clear the lower suspension arms and avoid scraping the road. Unfortunately, this restricted power, which no one noticed until Cobras were on sale. The cure involved fitting freer-flowing manifolds and mufflers, so the only complete and comprehensive answer was to recall all 8,000 1999 Cobras and do the work free of charge.

So for 2000, that's what they did. But it was such a huge workload for the relatively tiny SVT operation that

Above: The 2001 GT, still with the 4.6 V8 in SOHC cast-iron cylinder-block form, though with power now boosted to 260 bhp from the original 215 bhp.

Right: The standard GT did without the Cobra's independent rear suspension, though for most this wasn't an issue. Still a stunningly fast car.

Right: Jack Roush was a name still associated with tuned-up Mustangs in 2001, as this bodykit-equipped car testifies.

Below: Bigger rear spoiler, extended valance, side skirts and front spoiler, all hinted at the fact that this was a special Mustang.

Below right: The 4.6 liter V8, which had proved mildly disappointing when it replaced the old 5.0 in 1996, went on to show more of its potential.

they decided not to build any 2000 model year Cobras at all, with one exception. Actually, there were 300 of them. The Cobra R was an ultra-special version of the same car, ostensibly street legal, but really intended for the racetracks. The 4.6 V8 was dropped in favor of a 5.4 liter unit that was assembled especially for the R from a variety of Ford components. The cast-iron cylinder-block for example, was intended for trucks, but here fitted with four-valve DOHC aluminum heads. The cams were high-lift, the intake manifold specially made, and the con-rods made by Carillo from steel billets. Ford claimed 385 bhp at 5,700 rpm, and 385 lb. ft. at 4,500, making the 5.4 a

Below: Mustangs had long offered the choice of subtle or flash performance, and the case was no different in 2002, when the standard GT could be dressed up in stripes and wheels to make an impact.

highly efficient 71.3 bhp/liter. All this power was transmitted through a Tremec six-speed transmission, a four-inch aluminum driveshaft, and 3.55:1 rear axle. SVT engineers also scoured the world in search of top-name components, instead of adapting in-house parts: Eibach springs, Bilstein shocks, and Brembo brakes were all fitted.

Of course, as the Cobra R was intended as a racecar, there was little concession to comfort inside, with no air conditioning, sound system, or rear seat. Instead, it was all

Below right: Standard
4.6 liter V8, though in
Bullitt form it offered a
meatier torque curve. The
peak figure had barely
changed, but ninety-three
percent of it was available
at 2,200 rpm.

about performance and *Road & Track* confirmed that it
did indeed deliver. The hottest Cobra of all could reach
60 mph in 4.8 seconds, 100 mph in 10.9, and cross the
quarter-mile in just 13.2. Aerodynamics prevented it from
revving out in the high sixth gear, but change down to fifth
and the R would reach 170 mph. *Road & Track* pointed
out that a Corvette would be much easier to live with, not
to mention cheaper (the R was listed at $54,000) but the
fastest factory Mustang ever was still quite a car.

As for the standard Cobra, that returned for 2001, and
now with a guaranteed 320 bhp, which *Road & Track*
confirmed after testing one. They also described the
traction control system, which could actually be turned off
(via the "Power Start" switch) if drivers wanted to indulge
in tire-smoking starts. But if the system detected any
sideslip, it would automatically kick-in, turning down the

power and braking the affected wheel until the car was
pointing in the right direction—twenty-first century drivers,
however incompetent, were being saved from themselves.

Frank Bullitt of course, would have scorned such
"cheating" devices back in 1968. He was the detective
played by Steve McQueen in the movie of the same name,

and Mr. Bullitt smoked and squealed a dark green Mustang fastback through one of the longest car chases in cinematic history. Every car buff remembers that chase, which is probably why Ford offered a special edition "Bullitt" Mustang in 2001, in dark green, black, or blue. But it wasn't just a cosmetic special. The 4.6 V8 benefited from

Below: Chrome alloys, hood scoop, side scoops, and spoilers. This twenty-first century GT arguably more of a sports car than any of its predecessors.

twin 57 mm throttle bodies, a free-flowing exhaust, and aluminum intake manifold. On paper, these changes gave a scant five horsepower extra, and an even scanter 3 lb. ft. But those peak figures told only part of the story, for the Bullitt's torque curve was far fatter and flatter than that of the standard Mustang, offering ninety-three percent of the peak torque at just 2,200 rpm. It didn't have the Cobra's independent rear suspension, but the Bullitt was significantly quicker than a standard Mustang from low

Below: Look familiar? With its hood scoop, spoilers, and matt black panels, the 2003 Mach 1 Mustang was clearly inspired by the 1969 original.

speeds, and in any case did benefit from stiffer springs and a lower ride height, plus Tokico shocks—and with 1960s style five-spoke alloy wheels, fake air scoops, and bright red brake calipers, it looked quite special too.

Officially, the Bullitt was launched as a 2002 model, but there were few other changes for that year. As road testers would point out, all Mustangs really deserved the Cobra's all-independent suspension, but Ford stuck with the cheaper live rear axle for all lesser models. Not that it

Below: No doubts from the license plate as to the identity of this car! Twin exhaust outlets are a standard Mustang feature, from the GT upwards.

All on this page: Whether in red or blue, the 2003 Mach 1 still came with that matt black stripe, plus the Shaker hood, which shivered and shook, and reminded everyone that a real live V8 lay underneath.

Following page: The standard GT carried on, now sandwiched (in power terms) between the basic 3.8 liter V6 below it, with the Mach 1 and Cobra above.

seemed to worry the customers, who continued to sign on the dotted line in Ford showrooms in reasonably large numbers, while the Mustang remained the best selling ponycar of them all.

You had to be a fairly hard driver to be truly bothered by that live axle, and most folk weren't. They were more concerned about the New Edge styling, or deciding which option pack to choose. These had actually been greatly simplified of late, and from a possible 2,600 separate options, there were now just fifty option packs, which simplified the buying process and must have caused sighs of relief among Detroit production controllers. New options that year included a Mach 1000 sound system, with speed-sensitive volume control (slow from a high cruising speed to a traffic jam crawl, and the volume came down to suit), while the V6 Mustang now had sixteen-inch

alloy wheels as standard, though its looks could be further spruced up with the Sport Appearance Group.

The Fox-4 Mustang, truth be told, was nearing the end of its life, and these minor changes were intended to buoy up interest in a car that was wearing its near-decade in production very well. Ford had learnt that nostalgia sells, especially with a car as long-lived as the Mustang, so 2003 saw the return of the Mach 1. Like the original Mach 1, this one was more about appearance than extra performance. It did use the DOHC thirty-two-valve 4.6 V8, though here in 305 bhp form, not the full-house 320 bhp version fitted to the Cobra. But the Mach 1's real reason for being was to make a statement. Atop the hood

Above: A 2003 GT, minus the Mach 1's Shaker hood, seventeen-inch alloys, and other goodies, but looking pretty special nonetheless.

Opposite top: This is the SVT's interpretation of the Cobra for 2003.

Opposite bottom: Supercharging the Cobra took power up to 390 bhp.

was a massive Shaker scoop, which quivered and shook in sympathy with the V8 it was attached to. Serious muscle cars of the late 1960s had Shakers too, not to mention "Ram Air" induction—and yes, the 2003 Mach 1 had that too. There were also racing stripes, seventeen-inch alloy wheels, a prominent rear spoiler, and adjustable rear shocks. But unlike some of those original muscle cars, this Mach 1 couldn't be had in stripped-down form. It cost $5,000 more than the standard GT, and was only available with the Premium equipment group, which included a Mach 460 sound system and six-CD changer.

Despite which, the Mach 1 paid unashamed homage to the classic muscle car era, though if anyone thought the Mustang was drifting into "lifestyle" motoring, they need only look to the SVT Cobra, now supercharged for 2003

Above: The Shaker hood was a central feature of the new Mach 1, and it even offered Ram Air induction, another key word for muscle car buffs, and one that echoed from the late 1960s.

with 390 bhp and a six-speed manual transmission. Factory Mustangs had never been as powerful, or as expensive, as this before—Lee Iacocca's concept of "small-sporty" wasn't just thirty-nine years away from the 2003 Cobra, it was a whole lifetime.

They say life begins at forty, but the Mustang's fortieth anniversary also marked the final year for the Fox-4. Ford was upfront about the fact that a new Mustang was just around the corner, promoting the Mach 1 with the slogan "get one while you can." That year, the range started at $18,775 for the base coupe V6, while an SVT Cobra without options was listed at just over $35,000. There was

Above: Wide alloy wheels with low-profile tires were part of the Mach 1 package, plus adjustable rear shocks and spoiler.

a fortieth Anniversary option package, available as a coupe or convertible in Crimson Red, Black, or Oxford White. All three colors came with a Medium Parchement interior and Arizona Beige Metallic alloy wheels. There were stripes on the hood, lower door panels, and trunk lid, while inside

Above right: Still galloping
after all these years, the
pony logo was displayed
big and bold on the nose of
the 2003 Mustang.

the Mustang's fortieth was celebrated with appropriate
floor mats, four-way head restraints, a leather-covered shift
knob, stainless steel footrests and pedals, plus a few other
items. If that didn't appeal, the Pony Package on V6
Mustangs added sixteen-inch polished wheels, big
"Mustang" lettering across the rear end, a GT hood scoop,
and leather-covered steering wheel.

But these were baubles, intended to maintain interest
in the Fox-4 before it was replaced. Ford actually unveiled
the 2005 Mustang early, at the North American
International Auto Show in early 2004, well ahead of the
official on-sale date in the Fall. Just one glance at the all-
new Mustang gave it all away—it didn't just bear a family
resemblance to the 1964 Mustang, but looked more like a
twenty-first century version of exactly the same car. The
nose job, the round headlights, the big rectangular grille,
and the car's whole profile—all shouted 1960s Mustang

fastback. If purists pointed out that original fastbacks didn't have a rear quarter window, Ford could counter that the 1966 Shelby GT 350, the one bought by Hertz, did.

Not much was known about the fifth generation in early 2004, apart from the fact that it would still offer both V6 and V8 engines. Oh, and Ford already had an advertising slogan ready and waiting, one which paid homage to the engineers, designers, and marketeers who had come up with the ponycar idea in the first place: "Anybody can build a sports car," it went, "Only Ford can build a Mustang."

Above: By 2003, the Fox-4 Mustang was nearly a decade in production, though it didn't look it, so effective had the 1999 New Edge facelift been.

Right: Thirty-nine years on, and the Mustang had traveled far from its ponycar roots. But it is still one of America's best known marques.

MUSTANG TIMELINE 1964–2004

1964

April 17—Mustang launched to a rapturous reception. New concept of "small-sporty' combines sports car-like body with components from Falcon and Fairlane. Engine options include 170 cu. in. six, 260 cu. in. V8, 289 cu. in. V8. Good looks and low price make it an immediate hit, with over 400,000 sold in the first twelve months, making it one of the quickest-selling cars of all time. Three months after launch, performance 289 Hi-Po added, with 271 hp.
Beatlemania grips U.S. as the Fab Four fly in to Kennedy Airport
Nelson Mandela sentenced to life imprisonment in South Africa
President Lydon Johnson signs the Civil Rights Act

1965

Shelby GT 350 launched, a rough and ready racer for the road, stripped out to save weight, with stiffer suspension and a tuned 289 V8. Fast (0–60 mph in 6.5 seconds), noisy and difficult to drive on the limit, but the original Shelby becomes a legend. Ford launches the Mustang fastback 2+2, with same options as coupe and convertible, and fold down rear seats. It never sells as well as the other two, but acquires its own following.
Winston Churchill dies
U.S. troops go into battle in Vietnam for first time
First U.S. astronaut space walk

1966

Mustang's best year ever, over 600,000 cars sold, and the millionth ponycar rolls off the line. Three Ford factories are now turning out Mustangs as fast as possible. In an economic downturn, Ford stresses the economy of the basic six-cylinder Mustang, now more popular thanks to a base unit of 200 cu. in. and 120 hp. Meanwhile the Shelby GT 350 is softened and sanitized a little, and Hertz order 1,000 GT 350Hs to offer the meanest rental car of all time.

Julie Christie and Omar Sherif star in the movie *Dr. Zhivago*
Bob Dylan shocks the faithful by using an electric backing band
Chairman Mao proclaims Cultural Revolution

1967

Wider, heavier Mustang launched, to accommodate big-block V8s needed to keep up with the new ponycar opposition from GM and Chrysler, though it retains a strong family resemblance to the original. Top 390 V8 now offers a 15.2-second quarter-mile, but soon gets overtaken by rivals. Meanwhile, Shelby is offering the 428 cu. in. GT 500 with a claimed 355 hp, enough for 0–60 mph in 6.5 seconds and an estimated top speed of 128 mph.
Elvis Presley and Priscilla Beaulieu marry
Israel sweeps across Arab lands in the Six Day War
Race riots sweep U.S.

1968

California Special and High Country Special, limited editions of basic Mustang six, with Shelby-style add-ons, but the big news is Ford's own 428-engined Mustang, which finally caught up with the Camaro and Firebird. The Cobra Jet Mustang covered the quarter-mile in 13.56 seconds, 0–60 mph in 5.9 seconds. This follows Tasca Ford's 428-powered

dealer special KR ("King of the Road"), and a big-block Mustang is part of factory range for four years.

Martin Luther King is assassinated
Street fighting and strikes across France—President De Galle reimposes order
Russian tanks roll into Czechoslovakia as Soviets crush the Prague Spring

1969
Mustang facelifted with longer and wider bodyshell. SportsRoof replaces fastback, plus limited edition Boss 302 and 429, the former aimed at Trans Am racing, the latter a homologation special to qualify the special 429 V9 for NASCAR. Wide choice of engines includes 200 and 250 cu. in. sixes, plus 302 V8 (220 hp in 2-barrel form, 290 hp 4-barrel), 351 V8 (250 or 290 hp), 390 V8 (335 hp), 428 Cobra Jet (335 hp or 360 hp), and 429 V8 (375 hp).

Richard Nixon becomes U.S. President
John Lennon and Yoko Ono hold "bed in" for peace
Neil Armstrong is the first man on the moon

1970
Falling sales (to 300,000 Mustangs in 1969, 190,000 in 1970) see the engine range trimmed back. The final Shelbys are sold (production had ceased in 1969) and muscle car sales are hit by spiralling insurance costs, and safety and emissions legislation.

Final year for the Boss 302 and Boss 429, though the name lives on. Mustang Grande hardtop is maybe more in tune with the times, with luxury interior and soft suspension emphasised over performance.

First Jumbo Jet flight across the Atlantic
The Beatles split
Charles de Galle dies

1971
Biggest Mustang yet, 7 inches wider and 8 inches longer than the original, and around 500 lb. heavier. Radically raked SportsRoof receives mixed reviews, alongside convertible and coupe. 429 V8 (in cheaper production form) becomes a regular option with claimed 375 hp. Boss 351 and Mach 1 are new muscle Mustangs, though both can be had with the base 302 V8 to beat high insurance costs. Drag Pak (with 3.91 or 4.11:1 rear axles) aimed at drag racers.

Britain ditches pounds, shillings, and pence
Riots flare in Northern Ireland
Louis Armstrong dies

1972
Sales slump to an all-time low of 125,000, as U.S. buyers switch to smaller cars—Mustang looks out of tune with the times. Boss 351 and 429 V8 options are dropped, and for a while the top Mustang offers "only" 200 bhp SAE. 351HO (275 bhp) returns mid-

year in cleaned-up form, thanks to lower compression and milder cam timing—still manages 15.1 second quarter-mile and 0–60 mph in 6.6. Evaporative emissions equipment added to all cars.
President Nixon pays state visit to China, and is re-elected
Mark Spitz wins seven gold medals at the Munich Olympics
U.S. combat troops withdraw from Vietnam

1973
351HO is dropped, and Mustang lineup now consists of 250 six (80 bhp), 302 V8 (140 bhp), and 351 V8 (177 bhp 2-barrel, 248 bhp Cobra Jet 4-barrel). Other mechanical options (such as rear axle ratios) restricted by the need to smog test every combination. Sales recover slightly, partly thanks to a final surge of interest in the open-top Mustang, after Ford announces the convertible will die at the end of 1973. Sales had previously been slipping year on year, and this is now Ford's sole convertible.
Watergate scandal rocks the U.S.
Jackie Stewart retires from motor racing
Oil producing states announce a 70% increase in the price of oil

1974
Mustang II, radically downsized from 1973, 17 inches shorter and much lighter—based on Pinto components. Basic engine is a 2.3 liter four (for the

first time on a Mustang) with 2.8 liter V6 optional. No convertible, but two-door coupe and three-door hatchback, the latter in base or Mach 1 form (standard V6 with stripes and spoilers to give the appearance of a muscle car) and the coupe as a base or Ghia (replacing the Grande.) All are well-equipped (though more expensive than the full-size 1973 Mustang, and a sales hit—386,000 sold.
Richard Nixon resigns the Presidency
Alexander Solzhenitsyn receives the Nobel Prize
India detonates her first nuclear device

1975
V8 option added to Mustang II, the 302 cu. in. small-block in mild 122 bhp 2-barrel form with automatic transmission—0–60 mph 10.5 seconds. Heavier engine gives 60/40 weight distribution, but Ford works hard on suspension to give reasonable handling. Reborn V8 welcomed by media, but best selling Mustang remains the basic 2.3 liter four, followed by Ghia—Mach 1 and V8 lag behind. Optional MPG package promises 30 mpg, which counts for much in 1975.
Vietnam War ends as Siagon surrenders
Soccer star Pele joins the New York Cosmos
Handshakes in space as U.S. and U.S.S.R. astronauts meet

1976
Cobra II is a surprise hit. Intended as a limited edition, but customers like its stripes, spoilers, and

scoops so much (even with the 88 bhp four) that it becomes a regular production model. Supposed to evoke memories of the original Shelby GT 350, and 20,000 are sold, some with the 302 V8. Cobra II is either a hollow fake or clever piece of marketing, in tune with difficult times, depending on your viewpoint. Carroll Shelby gives the Cobra his personal seal of approval.

Concorde, the world's first supersonic airliner, carries its first passengers

Howard Hughes, the reclusive U.S. tycoon, dies

Jimmy Carter elected U.S. President

1977

Still no convertible, but for 1977 the T-top option offers a halfway house, with removable roof panels to give either hardtop weather protection or "wind in the hair." Simpler sunroofs are cheaper alternatives, while the Ghia Sports and Rally Appearance packages are other new options. But new CAFÉ regulations show up even the Mustang II to be a gas guzzler, at least in V8 form, and work proceeds on a more efficient replacement.

Space Shuttle makes its maiden flight

The first *Star Wars* movie hits the big screen

Elvis Presley dies

1978

Final year for Mustang II, with dressed-up King Cobra intended to repeat the success of Cobra II.

Bright colors, spoilers, alloy wheels, huge hood decal, together with standard 302 V8, four-speed manual transmission, competition suspension, power brakes and power steering. Fails to impress the buyers, and only 4,318 actually tick the option box, though the whole range does well, with over 190,000 sold. Whatever enthusiasts might think about Mustang II, the buyers loved it.

Argentina wins the World Cup

Louise Brown, the world's first test-tube baby, is born

Mass suicide by 913 members of the People's Temple, followers of Rev. Jim Jones

1979

Fox Mustang launched, much lighter, more aerodynamic and fuel-efficient than Mustang II, based on a shortened version of the Fairmont sedan platform. Wedge shaped body in two-door coupe and three-door hatchback form, though engines are carried over from Mustang II: 2.3 liter four, 2.8 liter V6, and 5.0 liter V8. Big news is 2.3 Turbo, offering near-V8 power, but with better fuel economy—Ford would persevere with this concept for seven years.

Revolution in Iran topples the Shah

Israel and Egypt sign peace treaty at the White House

Margaret Thatcher becomes Britain's first female Prime Minister

1980

Second oil crisis ensures that basic four-cylinder remains the most popular Mustang. Supply problems see V6 dropped in favor of ageing 3.3 liter (200 cu. in.) six while V8 downsized to 4.2 liters and comes with compulsory auto transmission. So four-cylinder turbo seen as performance flagship—limited edition SVO Turbo offers McLaren-tuned engine with 175 bhp, and $25,000 price tag, with ISMA-style bodykit, flared fenders, and BBS alloy wheels.

Millions face famine in East Africa

Iran and Iraq go to war

In Poland, Lech Walesa leads the new "Solidarity" union

1981

Fuel economy still dominates. Turbo dropped (both McLaren SVO and production line 150 bhp turbo), and V8 continues in 4.2 liter form with automatic transmission only. New five-speed manual for four-cylinder Mustangs, with economy overdrive ratio, while T-top (now renamed T-Roof) returns as a halfway house between hardtop and convertible, with twin glass panels and the same mix of hardtop and ragtop advantages. Four-cylinder Mustang still the most popular.

Prince Charles and Diana Spencer marry

Iran releases its U.S. hostages after 444 days in captivity

De Lorean sports car company collapses

1982

Big news. The Mustang begins its long climb back to muscle car status, with the return of the 5.0 liter V8 in 157 hp form with standard four-speed manual transmission. Fast (0–60 mph in 7 seconds) with Handling suspension, low-profile tires, and aluminum wheels, not to mention Traction-Lok differential and sporty add-ons. The new Mustang GT is also good value at $8,308. Ford's answer to the new fuel-injected Camaro delights the press. Performance is back.

Argentina invades the Falkland Islands

Sophia Loren is arrested for tax evasion

Israelis drive the PLO out of Beirut

1983

The convertible returns, the first fully open-top Mustang for ten years, in GLX or GT form with standard power hood and choice of 3.8 liter V6 or 5.0 liter V8. Over 20,000 sold in the first year, reflected pent-up demand for convertibles—it will become an increasingly important part of the Mustang range. Meanwhile, V8 boosted to 175 bhp and 245 lb. ft., to keep up with 190 bhp Camaro, and 2.3 Turbo returns with 145 bhp.

The "Hitler Diaries" are published—they were found to be a hoax

Peace protesters march against U.S. Cruise missiles in the U.K.

U.S. Marines invade Grenada

1984

Ford celebrates Mustang's 20th anniversary with a "GT 350" special edition (Carroll Shelby is not pleased, and takes Ford to court for use of "his" name—he loses) while latest intercooled SVO Turbo has 175 bhp. The 3.8 liter V6 gets fuel injection and there's a new touring V8 option, with 165 bhp and standard automatic. ChiPS opt to buy Mustang V8 patrol cars.

First warnings about the greenhouse effect and the depletion of the ozone layer

Ronald Reagan elected U.S. President

1985

Another power boost for the GT V8, to 210 bhp and 265 lb. ft. from a new camshaft, high-capacity headers, and low-friction roller tappets. Quarter-mile in 14–15 seconds and 0–60 mph in 6–7 seconds, slightly quicker than IROC-Z Camaro, which has more power but less torque. Performance now back to 1960s muscle car levels, and the GT retains its traditional four-barrel carburetor (though this is its final year). The cruiser V8 is boosted to 180 bhp.

Mikhail Gorbachev is new Soviet leader

Live Aid rock concert manages to raise £40 million for famine relief

Reagan and Gorbachev agree to cut their nuclear arsenals by 50%

1986

Mustang GT V8 finally gets fuel injection, a sequential multi-point system offering slightly less power but a fatter torque curve. Also more fuel-efficient, allowing the top Mustang to avoid the gas guzzler tax, though meanwhile the top Camaro has 230 bhp. Ford's trump card is that the Chevrolet costs hundreds of dollars more than a Mustang GT, which remains the best-value performance car in 1980s America.

Space shuttle Challenger explodes on take-off

Statue of Liberty celebrates 100th birthday

British Government launches its biggest-ever health campaign, against AIDS

1987

Ford rejects plans for an all-new Mustang (too expensive) while the public rejects the notion of sharing a design with Mazda. So the Fox soldiers on, with a facelift bringing a smoother look for 1987, while keen buyers can specify the full-power 5.0 liter V8 on the plain-looking LX—lighter than the flashy GT, slighter faster, and $1,500 cheaper. V8 now produces 225b hp, but sticks with 5.0 liters (despite rumors of a forthcoming 5.7 liter).

Lt-Col. Oliver North is at the center of the Irangate scandal

Hurricane-force winds batter the south of England

Reagan and Gorbachev sign a treaty to cut nuclear arsenals

1988

The V6, touring V8, and turbocharged four all dropped, leaving just two engine options—90 bhp four and 225 bhp V8. Despite less choice, 1988 is a good year, with 214,000 Mustangs sold. Steve Saleen is offering modified Mustangs with Ford's blessing, concentrating on suspension, interior, and bodykit. Despite speculation, there's no sign of a 250 bhp 5.7 liter Mustang, and Ford decides not to go ahead with a 400 bhp twin-turbo for the pony car's 25th anniversary.

Turin Shroud is declared to be a fake

Unrest grows in Communist Eastern Europe

1989

T-Roof option dropped, as the full convertible Mustang goes from strength to strength, with over 40,000 sold this year. Ford fails to capitalize on the ponycar's 25th birthday, apart form a small dashboard plaque. Steve Saleen offers a tuned Mustang for the first time, claiming 292 bhp for the $35,000 SSC—*Car and Driver* record a 0–60 mph time of 5.9 seconds and a 14.2-second standing-quarter. The SSC also uses reinforcements to stiffen up the Fox's flexible body.

Berlin Wall demolished as Eastern Europe transforms
Thousands of students are massacred in Tianamen Square, Peking
Electron-Positron Collider begins operation in Switzerland

1990

Limited edition convertible in Deep Emerald Jewel Green with white leather interior and ragtop, GT alloy wheels, and luggage rack. Most ordered as automatics and some maintain that this (based on the standard LX convertible) was Ford's 25th anniversary special. The Mustang is increasingly referred to as a "retro" car, offering a 1960s muscle car experience in 1990, though the little four-cylinder unit is just as popular.

Nelson Mandela freed from prison in South Africa
Mikhail Gorbachev wins the Nobel Peace Prize
Iraq invades Kuwait

1991

Twin-plug ignition for the 2.3 liter four boosts power to 105 bhp and cuts emissions, not to mention returning 30 mpg on the highway. New 16-inch five-spoke alloy wheels with 225/55 tires spruce it up. Meanwhile, the V8 is unchanged in 225 bhp/300 lb. ft. form. But sales dip to 99,000 (the worst yet) as the Fox begins to look outdated next to Japanese coupes and the Camaro. Still good value though, at $13,000 for the V8, and only a little over $10,000 for the basic four-cylinder coupe.

Abolition of apartheid in South Africa
Civil war in Yugoslavia
Operation Desert Storm drives Iraq out of Kuwait

1992

With a new Mustang on the horizon, sales slump again, to less than 80,000, setting a new low for the ponycar. Increasingly seen as a retro car, with its live axle, drum rear brakes, and lack of ABS. So convertible sales continue to thrive (23,000 this year) while the two-door coupe continues to slide (16,000). Engine choices split 50/50 between four and V8 as the Mustang continues to sell to distinct markets. Shelby Automobile Club launches its Shelby AAC Mk1 Mustang, which is almost as bumpy and raucous as the original.

Earth Summit held in Rio
Bill Clinton elected as U.S. President
European Union—Maastrict Treaty signed

1993
Final year interest for the Fox Mustang centers around the SVT-developed Mustang Cobra. This has the 5.0 liter V8 tuned to 235 bhp, with bigger valves and 70 mm throttle body, among other things, in an attempt to close the performance gap with the GM ponycars. Upgraded transmission, brakes, and suspension, but Cobra still can't match a top Camaro or Firebird. Limited edition convertibles in Canary Yellow or Oxford White mark the end of Fox production.
Movie *Schindler's List* gives a shocking account of the holocaust
Bomb rocks the World Trade Center, New York
Velvet Revolution in Czechoslovakia

1994
Fox-4 Mustang launched, with all-new body/chassis based on same basic mechanical layout. Quieter, more comfortable, and more curvaceous than Fox, and the body is significantly stiffer, designed from the outset to have a convertible option. There's no hatchback, so the choice is between a ragtop or two-door coupe. The four-cylinder option is replaced by a 145 bhp 3.8 liter V6, while the 5.0 liter V8 carried over, now with 215 bhp.
Nelson Mandela elected as the President of South Africa
IRA ceasefire lifts peace hopes in Northern Ireland
Genocide committed in Rwanda

1995
GTS coupe seeks to fill gap between base V6 and full-power GT, with the V8 engine but less equipment, saving $1,000. More relevant to enthusiasts is the SVT Cobra, with 240 bhp from the familiar 5.0 liter, with SVT's compliant suspension (relatively soft springs with good damping) A limited edition 5.7 liter Cobra R makes that 300 bhp (this is really a racecar) and the Mustang chosen as the Indy 500 pace car for the third time in its career.
Israel/Palestine sign peace treaty in Washington
Earthquake devastates the city of Kobe, Japan
Financial scandal in London when Barings Bank collapses

1996
Long-awaited new V8 arrives in Mustang, the 4.6 liter unit, already seen in Ford sedans. Standard spec (SOHC, cast-iron cylinder block) offered 215 bhp, but SVT Cobra comes with hand-built version (DOHC, 32 valves, alloy block) and 305 bhp. Despite early reliability problems, this is best selling Cobra yet. Less successful is a new removable hardtop option for the convertible, which attracts only 500 orders.
U.S. tobacco company Liggett agrees to pay for treatment of smokers
Russia pulls out of Chechnya
U.S. fires cruise missiles at Iraq

1997

Sales slump, from 185,000 in 1995 to just 108,000 in 1997, with standard GT suffering most—base V6 is the best selling Mustang. PATS anti-theft system standard across the range, along with a bigger radiator, and new 17-inch alloy wheels optional on GT. Cobra still selling well in convertible or coupe form. Steve Saleen offers the chance to humiliate Camaro Z28 owners with the Saleen S-351: 5.7 liter Windsor V8 with new cam, bigger valves, and throttle body plus modified engine management—claims 371 bhp.

Kyoto Protocol Convention on climate change
"Dolly the sheep" is the world's first cloned animal
Japan faces economic crisis

1998

Sales bounce back, with 175,000 Mustangs sold this year—now outsells Camaro and Firebird combined. Road tests show the ponycar to be less of a serious sports car than the General Motors twins (and even the Cobra can't quite match a Z28 on acceleration), but it's more fun and easier to live with. Standard GT boosted to 225 bhp, thanks to revised and cleaned up exhaust ports, and 290 lb. ft. The Cobra sticks with 305 bhp.

E-mail and internet fast growing in popularity
Hurricane Mitch kills 9,000 in Central America
Peace accords in Northern Ireland and Palestine

1999

Facelift for Fox-4, when "New Edge" styling sharpens it up, giving a tougher and more aggressive look. More power across the range, with 190 bhp V6, 260 bhp V8 (bigger valves, higher lift cam), and 320 bhp for the DOHC Cobra. Cobra also has independent rear suspension and far better handling, thirty-five years after Ford promised this as an option on the original Mustang. Traction control is a new option on all Mustangs, using the ABS system to tame unwanted wheelspin.

First round-the-world balloon flight
Vladimir Putin succeeds President Yeltsin in Russia
NATO air strikes on Serbia

2000

All 1999 Cobras recalled (8,000 of them), because of power deficit from squeezed exhaust system—new freer-flowing manifolds and mufflers needed to cure it. No mainstream Cobras are built this year, but the limited edition Cobra R did make it, with special 5.4 liter V8 (DOHC four-valve heads on a cast-iron block) with claimed 385 bhp/385 lb. ft. and Tremec six-speed manual transmission. Standing-quarter 10.9 seconds, 0–60 mph 4.8 seconds.

International Space Station launched
George Bush elected President, but doubt over the narrow margin
Global warming conference at the Hague fails

2001

Standard Cobra returns, now with full 320 bhp present and correct, and traction control which could be switched off to allow wheelspin starts. Limited edition Bullitt Mustang based on standard GT in dark green, blue, or black. Tuned 4.6 V8 (twin 57 mm throttle bodies, free-flowing exhaust, and aluminum intake manifold) with fatter torque curve gives noticeably better acceleration. Stiffer springs, lower ride height, and Tokico shocks also feature.

"Mad cow disease" spreads through Europe
9/11—hijacked planes crash into the World Trade Center killing thousands
Enron bankruptcy scandal in U.S.

2002

Few changes, though V6 gets a slight power boost to 193 bhp and 225 lb. ft. Still no sign of independent rear suspension on the non-Cobra Mustangs, but it doesn't appear to be holding back sales. The base Mustang now has 16-inch alloy wheels as standard, with Sport Appearance group optional—options are now offered in groups, not individually. One new option is the Mach 1000 sound system with automatic speed-sensitive volume control.

International Criminal Court established
Global warming causes collapse of Larsen B ice shelf in Antartica
WorldCom is the biggest bankruptcy in U.S. history

2003

Mach 1 Mustang returns, with all the styling cues of the 1969 original—Shaker hood scoop, Ram Air, racing stripes, rear spoiler, and 17-inch alloy wheels. Also fitted with the Cobra's DOHC 4.6 V8, but here in 305 bhp, not full 320 bhp, form. Costs $5,000 more than GT, partly because of compulsory Premium equipment group, which includes Mach 460 sound system and six-CD changer. Meanwhile, SVT Cobra now supercharged, with 390 bhp and six-speed transmission.

U.S.-led forces invade and occupy Iraq
A heatwave scorches Europe
Worldwide protests against the invasion of Iraq

2004

Mustang's 40th anniversary, celebrated with special option package on coupes or convertibles in Crimson Red, Black, or Oxford White. Medium Parchment interior and Beige Metallic alloy wheels, exterior stripes, and various interior add-ons. This is the final year for Fox-4, and Ford promotes the Mach 1 with the slogan "get one while you can." Ford unveils the 2005 Mustang early, and it shows clear inspiration from the 1960s Shelbys—the fifth generation Mustang will make the most of 40 years of heritage.

Libya ends its nuclear program
Uprisings in Iran against U.S.-led forces
Space probes on Mars find evidence of water

Index

Picture Credits

All photographs courtesy and © Garry Stuart except for pages 8-9, 164-171, 174-175, 184-187, 190-201, 204-229, 230-231, 236-237, 242-249, 250-253, 254-259, 264-267, 272-275, 284-287, 290-293, 318-319 which are © Chrysalis Images

Acknowledgments
The photographer, Garry Stuart would like to thank *Dale Richardson & Martha Richards* of Greeley, Colorado for their significant contribution to this book by tracking down many fine examples of Mustangs in the Denver area for photography.

Also thanks to master restorer of Shelby Mustangs *Ron Holland* for access to his fine collection.

Thanks also to the members of *The Early Mustang Club of Denver* and to the *Mustang Club of Loveland* and all the other owners who kindly allowed their cars to be photographed.

Many thanks also to the *5 Valley Mustang Club of Missoula Montana* and all who attended the *24th Annual International Mustang* meet, for their hospitality and allowing their cars to be photographed for this book. (www.mustanglovers.com)